Fairways of Life

Fairways of Life

Wisdom and Inspiration from the
Greatest Game

New York Times and *USA Today* best-selling coauthor
of *Chicken Soup for the Soul of America* and
Golf Channel Personality

Matthew E. Adams

Foreword by Arnold Palmer

Copyright © 2006 Matthew E. Adams

All inquiries should be addressed to:
Sports Media Group
An imprint of Ann Arbor Media Group, LLC
2500 S. State Street
Ann Arbor, MI 48104

Library of Congress Cataloging-in-Publication Data

Adams, Matthew E., 1964-
  Fairways of life : wisdom and inspiration from the greatest game / Matthew E. Adams ; foreword by Arnold Palmer.
    p. cm.
  ISBN-13: 978-1-58726-295-1 (hardcover : alk. paper)
  ISBN-10: 1-58726-295-9 (hardcover : alk. paper)
1. Golf--United States--Anecdotes. 2. Golfers--United States--Anecdotes. I. Title.

GV967.A33 2006
796.352--dc22

                                        2005025114

Printed and bound in the United States of America.

10 09 08 07 06   1 2 3 4 5

To Donna

"As you walk down the fairway of life you must smell the roses, for you only get to play one round."

∽ Ben Hogan

Contents

ৰ৴

The Front Nine

The Back Nine

Foreword

The sounds of crashing waves and a gentle yet persistent wind at my back greet me as I tee up my ball on the first hole of the Peninsula Papagayo Golf Course at the Four Seasons Resort in Costa Rica. The beauty of this sliver of land, jutting out into the Pacific Ocean on the northwest coast of Costa Rica, is almost overwhelming, yet I had to put aside such agreeable distractions to concentrate on the task at hand.

My purpose for being here is to ceremoniously open Peninsula Papagayo Golf Club and welcome it into the growing family of courses designed by Palmer Course Design. To date, they number almost three hundred golf projects. It is always a bit of a strange feeling to play a new course for the first time. It is a mixed sensation, with both the excitement of introducing a new course to the world and the accompanying trepidation that comes from leaving your mark on this earth with the hope that it will live up to your expectations and your client's. I am happy to report that Peninsula Papagayo achieves these goals and more.

My design goals with Peninsula Papagayo were the same as they are for virtually all of my golf courses all over the world—to design a course both challenging and fun for a broad range of golfing abilities while staying true to the genuine, traditional, and sound design concepts of the game. I did not invent these cornerstone concepts, having benefited greatly in observing them at great golf courses all over the world like the Old Course at St. Andrews, Augusta National, Pebble Beach, Ballybunion Old, and many others . . . I dare say a few of my own as well, such as Bay Hill and the one here at Peninsula Papagayo. To me, a golfing experience on a great golf course should be about more than simply what score you post. It should be the embodiment of a full spectrum of emotions ranging from dealing with adversity to the joy of accomplishment.

I believe I was inspired by the incredible beauty of this piece of land, perhaps the best site we have ever had on which to place a golf course. Yet thoughts about playing a golf course and how it reflects the "playing" of life continue to drift through my mind as I play this day.

When my friend Matt Adams asked me to write the foreword for this book, this day and the reflections it inspired instantly came to mind as an appropriate starting point.

After eight holes, I am 1-over par and standing on the tee box at the par-5, 525-yard eighteenth hole (I started my round on the tenth hole). The landing area is fairly broad and slopes slightly right to left down toward the ocean. The slope can be of great benefit in gaining additional roll on a tee shot, which is particularly important if the hole is playing into the wind, as it is today.

I hit one of my best drives of the day. It sails, with a slight draw, down the right side of the fairway, catching the top of the slope and settling some 245 yards from the green, atop a large hill some 50 feet above the green, dead in the center of the fairway. As I reach my tee shot I have to pause to take in the beauty of this locale. The views of the Pacific from this perch are even more spectacular than I remember from when we hiked through this rugged land with a machete and a sketch pad. This is one of those occasions when you feel your spirit lifted. You feel like anything is possible. I take a deep breath as if to try and breathe in the essence of this time and place.

As I surveyed my options—to lay up or go for it in two—my mind is thinking birdie, at least, and maybe even an eagle. The pin is center cut, the green is receptive, and my position high above the green, combined with a very gentle sea breeze and the natural contour of the land from right to left, would only help my shot run onto the green. A classic "go for it" situation.

But my golfing experience tells me that any abandonment of reason, prudence, and course management can quickly bring your heightened expectations back down to earth and result in a bogey, or worse. You see, while the approach shot looked fairly straightforward, this is a new golf course, and any number of hazards could easily reveal themselves to a less-than-perfect shot. A conservative approach shot, perhaps some sixty to eighty yards short of the green, would leave a very manageable third shot to reach the green in regulation.

It is amazing, isn't it, how much golf truly is a reflection of life? I have spent most of my life feeling like I am standing over approach shots like this, situated high above a waiting green and a thoroughly accessible pin for a certain birdie. Yet life does not always give you birdies, and often a strong wind or unforeseen hazard can derail even the best-laid plans. I am convinced that the lessons taught to me by many people, particularly my father, "Deacon" Palmer, and the lessons taught to me by a lifetime of golf have helped me to deal both with the adversities and successes of life and golf.

My dad taught me to remember that I was not the only person to inhabit this earth, and that I should treat everyone with the same respect and dignity with which I hoped they would treat me. He taught me the value of hard work, commitment, dedication, and loyalty. He helped me to see that no man stands alone, and that the day you start to believe that you are better than your fellow man, well, then I guess you truly are alone.

The game of golf has taught me the value of perseverance and imagination, of having a game plan and knowing who you are. It has revealed to me more than a lifetime's worth of its universal truths.

Since I have lived much of my life in the public eye, most of my triumphs and tribulations have played out before the masses.

I have felt my admirers cheer with me as I amassed seven professional majors and ninety-two more worldwide victories in my career. Perhaps even more importantly, I've felt them cry with me as I've dealt with life's adversities, facing not only with the loss of golf tournaments but also far more substantive matters such as the loss of my wife, Winnie, to cancer in 1999 and my battle with prostate cancer.

Now, as I stand on the eighteenth fairway at Peninsula Papagayo Golf Club, I have a 7-iron in my hand, prepared to begin my pre-shot routine. A familiar thought enters my mind. While the 7-iron would be a much safer shot to play, a heroic 3-wood would certainly be more fun.

Ultimately, isn't that what it is all about—getting the most out of life, contributing to the world in whatever way I can, and having *fun* doing it?

I slide the 7-iron back into the bag. With my mind and body free of reservation, I take an aggressive swing at the ball with my 3-wood. The ball rockets off the club face on a direct line toward the pin. Elated by the precision of the strike, I watch with great anticipation as it sails towards the target. Just thirty yards from the green, the ball is pushed slightly off-line by a sizable Pacific gust, landing it in a greenside bunker on the left side of the green.

Once again, the game of golf and the game of life present me with a challenge, and an opportunity. I can't wait to meet them both, head on.

I hope you enjoy this book as much as I have.

Arnold Palmer

2005

Preface

❧

I have spent over twenty years working in various aspects of the golf industry, from golf club manufacturing to golf media and, more recently, golf course operations. It is in this last capacity that I have found a particularly satisfying life balance. Working in the golf industry in New England, where I live, means that we have at least six months every year to invest our passions in something other than golf, for there is not a lot of golf being played under snow (except for the diehard fanatics). So I turn my interest to writing and research while the cold winter winds howl outside my walls.

Fairways of Life is the fifth book I have authored. In total, my books have sold over one million copies, which suggest some pretty impressive stuff. To me it is not, really. All of my previous books (except for 2005's *Fast and Lean Racing Cookbook*, with Robin Dallenbach) have been coauthored with Jack Canfield and Mark Victor Hansen as part of the *Chicken Soup for the Soul* series. I have more respect and gratitude to Jack and Mark than I can express. They were the ones who believed in me. They taught me the power of messages that are inspiring and how they can change lives. They showed me what it means to be an author working on a book series that has sold over seventy-five million books over the last fifteen years. Now *that* is something to be impressed with.

Yes, the books that I helped craft did well and were bestsellers, but their success depended as much upon the immense brand awareness generated by the *Chicken Soup for the Soul* title as upon the contribution of a coauthor such as I. I like to view myself as a realist, and I understand how that dynamic works. I cannot tell you how many times someone has asked me what books I have authored, and exclaim, after I tell them, "Oh, I have read that." So much for remembering the author, I guess. Perhaps this happens because the *Chicken Soup* books are compilations. It is generally assumed that *Chicken Soup* authors simply edit the work of others, and there is some truth to that. However, Jack and Mark have established a high standard for the stories they choose, and what an author of one of their books really ends up doing is writing (in the first person) about the wonderful experiences of other people who may not necessarily be writers. In the end, it is an extremely rewarding experience to author a *Chicken Soup for the Soul* book. The significance of the experience really hits home when you begin to receive letters from readers who tell you how one of your stories changed their lives.

My first book with Jack and Mark was *Chicken Soup for the Soul of America*, which was written immediately after the terrorist attacks of September 11, 2001. That book benefited the New York Area Relief Fund, and I can tell you that creating it was by far the most humbling experience of my life, save perhaps the birth of my children. I was deeply struck by the innate goodness of people who came together to help others in a time of profound crisis. Perhaps it is a natural balance, but I found that at the same time as we were exposed to the very worst of humanity, we also saw humanity's best in those that responded. As a writer, I came to partially understand the silent stoicism of our fathers' generation, who routinely said little of their experiences at war unless they were speaking with another who was there. I was dispatched to Ground Zero immediately after the attack, and I (as we all were) was so overcome with a myriad of emotions, I did not know how to craft them into words. How does one describe the indescribable? What common frame of reference can one have with anyone else who was not there—the burning soot that stung your nostrils, the remnants of the Towers standing in crippled, ghostly defiance, the removal of the victims? I could

Fairways of Life

find no common frame of reference from which to begin. Yet among this immense grief and loss there was still hope. It was the resiliency of the people, like flowers growing up through cracks in the rubble, that ultimately struck me. It was the willingness to love when it would be easier to simply hate. Ultimately, it was these messages of love and hope that spoke for themselves.

And so, through that experience and that book, Jack and Mark gave me my first lessons in the magic and power of *Chicken Soup for the Soul* and helped me define myself as an author. Those lessons, as I saw it, were elementary and critical, yet too often forgotten or ignored. They taught me to trust in the goodness of others. To help them see the beauty and potential they possess. To help them find happiness and love. And finally, that no matter how much the world bombards us with negative messages, our charity of spirit still needs to be fed, and it is natural to seek out a source for stories of goodness, hope, and perspective.

Being a *Chicken Soup for the Soul* author, touring the country speaking to groups about how to live happy, productive, and empowered lives, and working for over twenty years in the golf industry may seem on the surface to be conflicting activities, yet to me the two could not be more similar. Golf is a game of beauty, solace, companionship, exercise (physically and mentally), and fun. It is the consummate ideal of that which I speak about from day to day, which I suppose can be boiled down into a philosophy of making that which you are passionate about into your life's purpose. Too many people live their lives as a dichotomy of that which they love and that which they hate. Most justify this imbalance by claiming that without the part they despise, they could not have the part they love. I simply do not believe this, and much of this book works to dispel this myth, using the game of golf as the basis for discovery.

If there are wisdom and insight in this book, I do not feel that it comes from me, but from the rich history of the game and the individuals who have shaped it. My observations and opinions come from my training with two of the best teachers and philosophers of human potential that exist today, Jack Canfield and

Mark Victor Hansen. I have tried in this work to combine the universal messages of hope, perspective, perseverance, and love that I have learned from them with the inspiration and empowerment I have felt in my life around the greatest game.

Some may assume that writing a book is a lot like golf, and that the more you do it (and the more success you have had doing it), the easier it becomes. With me, that is not the case. I find that writing a book is like trying to put a pane of glass back together after it has been smashed into a million pieces. It is delicate, trying, time-consuming, and full of stress and anxiety. It is the embodiment, really, of all of the things that I strive to help people minimize or eliminate from their lives! In that regard the process is ironic, but the rewards of having a forum to express my wonderment at the game's endless life lessons and the hope that maybe a small part of this book will touch the life of another make the long hours well worth the effort.

This is not a book about how to play better *golf*. It is a book about how to play better *life*. I hope it provides you with a window into the timeless wisdom of the game and that you enjoy this book for many years to come.

Good golfing,

Matthew E. Adams
2006

Acknowledgments

༄

While this book may bear the name of a single author, it is certainly not the result of a single person's effort. I am blessed to be surrounded by extraordinary people who are an endless source of love, support, creativity, and expertise. As it is my belief that we are all only as good as those with whom we surround ourselves, I am humbled to be in the company of those who made this book a reality and the countless more that have touched my life—all those whom space here has prohibited me from naming specifically.

To my dear wife Donna and my boys Austin and CJ, thank you for your unconditional support and the selfless sacrifice you have made in allowing me to exhaust hundreds of hours in devotion to the writing of this book; that was really time that belonged to you.

To my mother and father, Joan and Bob Adams, for instilling in me the value of hard work, tenacity, and never settling for another person's judgment of what heights I should aspire to. My father died too young, but his impact on this world will be long felt. Also, to my five brothers and sisters, Mary Ann, Bob, Jr., Michael, Joan, and Cathy, and to their spouses and children, thank you for being an endless source of inspiration.

Thank you to my publisher, Skip Dewall of Sports Media Group, for seeing the merits of this book and to Bob Kraut for bringing us together.

To Jeff and Patty Aubery for introducing me to the life-changing world of *Chicken Soup for the Soul* and to the incredible world of publishing. Without your support, I would not be an author.

To Jack Canfield, my mentor. Thank you for taking the time to indulge my dreams. I believe everyone is put on this earth for a specific purpose, and I have never met another who so clearly understands the role his Creator intended him to play.

To Jeff Hymes, Lee Siegel, Eric Saperstein, and Adam Barr of the Golf Channel for giving me my start with the network, and to all the other hardworking people there that I have the pleasure to work with. Thank you for allowing me to live out my life philosophy of doing what you love and loving what you do. The Golf Channel is a place of talent and passion. I am honored to be a small part of it.

To my wonderful and talented staff, John, Robin, Scott, and others. Without your expertise and tireless work ethic, I would not be able to balance it all.

To Jim Hansberger, Julian Bunn, Scott Austin, Nat C. Rosasco, Bill Jesse, Tony Ragano, and the countless others who taught me the inner workings of the game and business of golf. You have been my teachers on a path that has fulfilled my life. Also, to Art and Norm Cummings, who gave me my start in combining my love of golf and media. To Wayne, Thomas, Doc, Rob, Steve, Terry, Ed, Heidi, Fran, Billy, Mike, Geoff, Fritz, Chris, Jamie, Jocko, Fred, Dave, Buzz, Jim, Roy, Honey, Brian, Don, George, Tony, Mark, Paul, Allen, Rich, Cam, Carl, Casey, Dan, Tim, Tom, Kelly, Doug, John, and many, many more for being dear friends and inspiring golf partners. You have helped me learn that there is more to golf, and life, than missing a putt, although I appreciate all of the gimme putts you have mercifully granted.

To my friends and teachers at the Shepaug Valley Regional High School and Providence College for teaching me that real education is as much about what happens outside the classroom as within it.

To the legendary Arnold Palmer, for agreeing to impart to all of us his wisdom in this book's foreword. I am so honored and humbled that a man of your accomplishments would consider being a part of my book that I am without adequate words to express my gratitude, except to say thank you.

To the distinguished group of men who agreed to provided testimonials for this book, Tim Finchem, Donald Trump, Jack Canfield, Roger Warren, Billy Donovan, and Tom Drennen. Thank you for your vision and belief. While the collective mountain of accomplishments you have attained may seem impossible to top, the life's work of each of you provides an inspiring path for others to follow.

To my sample readers and story contributors, Herb Stevens, Bob Adams Jr., Jason Pannone, Matt Fitzgerald, Ed Holda, Norm Cummings, George White, Mark Cubbedge, and Stuart Jordan. Thank you for your time, talent, and indulgence. Thank you also to the Trinity Repertory Theater in Providence, Rhode Island, for allowing me a place of solitude and reflection where much of this book was written (while waiting for my young son, Austin, to finish his rehearsals as Tiny Tim in the annual performance of Charles Dickens' *A Christmas Carol*).

It is, no doubt, quite obvious that it is impossible to name all of the individuals who have played a part in making this book, and the life I enjoy, a reality. Suffice it to say that I am eternally grateful to all of you, mentioned by name here or not, for your love, friendship, kindness, insight, and wisdom. I hope that this book can serve as a testament to the way your lives have made this world a better place.

Introduction

ॐ

Harry Vardon and Ted Ray were imposing figures in the world of golf in 1913. The distinguished-looking Vardon, a five-time winner of the (British) Open Championship (he would win it a record sixth time, in 1914), was the best player in the world, the Tiger Woods of his era. Ray, the reigning British Open champion, was a large, thick man with a walrus mustache. He was distinctive for his massive drives, making him the John Daly of his day. The two were in the midst of an extensive tour through the United States, where the Brits would team up against anyone foolish enough to challenge them. Entering the U.S. Open at The Country Club in Brookline, Massachusetts, the two had built a record of forty-one wins and no losses. Their mere presence at the relatively young U.S. Open was a great boost for the tournament's prestige.

The two stood in stark contrast to Francis Ouimet, an unknown twenty-year-old amateur golfer from a working-class family. Ouimet had grown up across the street from The Country Club, and as a child he would peer through the trees for hours, watching the wealthy and privileged members play the game. Golf captured Ouimet's fascination early on, and he would often sneak onto The Country Club grounds, playing a few holes with a single golf club that belonged to his brother. By the time he turned eleven, Ouimet had started caddieing at The Country Club, furthering his education about the game and the nuances of the grand old course. He developed into a solid player and entered the 1913 U.S. Open principally for the chance to see his hero, Vardon, up close.

Through the first two rounds, the tournament played out as scripted. Vardon and Ray were at the top of the leaderboard, with a host of accomplished players in contention. Ouimet's play was respectable, if unnoticed, and he kept himself within striking distance of the lead. In fact, by the end of the third round, the overachieving Ouimet would find himself tied with Vardon and Ray atop the leaderboard.

Midway through the tournament the weather began to turn foul, and by the morning of the fourth and final round, The Country Club was saturated, making the already long and difficult golf course even more formidable. Usually a situation such as this would be an advantage for the sage professionals, Vardon and the long-hitting Ray, yet through the muck and tension the two champions struggled home with 79s. Ouimet, who seemed remarkably unfettered by the gravity of his position, likewise struggled through difficult conditions, and it took an assertive birdie on the seventeenth hole to insure his position in the three-way play-off the following day against Vardon and Ray to determine the U.S. Open champion.

The morning of the play-off dawned under gray skies and a light mist. It wasn't until Ouimet was standing at the first tee, looking out at the thousands of spectators lining the hole, about to start a play-off against the two best players in the world, that he realized the significance of the position he was in. However, that revelation was lost on his fellow competitors. Vardon and Ray, and presumably most everyone else, had already decided that the championship would be determined between them. The two legends hardly took notice of the young amateur.

Ouimet was a humble, unassuming young man. So much so, in fact, that he asked Eddie Lowery, a small-for-his-age ten-year-old kid from his neighborhood to caddie for him during the championship. The two boys standing on the tee box, next to Vardon and Ray and their respective caddies, looked markedly unusual.

As he had done through the first four rounds of the tournament, Ouimet seemed unaffected by the crushing pressure that seemed to be slowly consuming his seasoned competition. His cool could be chalked up partly to his youth and inexperience; not having been in such a position before, he did not have a point of reference on which to draw. Yet, his mental state was also due to his solid upbringing, his sense of having nothing to lose, and his own steely-eyed determination.

After the first nine holes, all three men were tied with scores of 38. At the par-3 tenth hole, Ouimet would take the lead after Vardon and Ray three-putted for bogeys. Ouimet would continue his inspired play while a stunned and visibly shaken Vardon kept it close. Ray, however, fell two shots behind Ouimet by the sixteenth hole and effectively gave up the fight. At the par-4 seventeenth, Vardon attempted to gain the advantage by cutting his drive close to the dogleg in the hope of a better position on the approach shot. The result of his gamble was that his drive landed in a fairway bunker, leading to a bogey. Ouimet, with the heart of a lion, split the fairway with his drive. A laserlike approach shot set up a fifteen-foot birdie putt that Ouimet drilled home, icing his victory and the biggest upset in the history of the game.

The inspiring victory of Francis Ouimet, the youth from the "wrong side of the tracks" against a field of world-famous professionals and amateur golfers of power and means provides the ultimate example of the game of golf as a metaphor for the most important game of all, the game of life.

Ouimet's triumph was front-page news. Not only is it credited with being the impetus for the explosive and sustained growth of golf in the United States, but the victory by the young man who would not give up has also inspired millions to have the courage to believe in themselves, regardless of the field of battle, and not to allow their level of accomplishment and success to be defined by the limited view of others.

Such is the promise and eternal optimism of the game of golf.

Unlike any other sport, golfers embrace the game as a lifestyle and not merely as an avocation. The best selling golf books have always been those that capture a broader, almost mystical application of the universal truths of the game. This book is intended to use the timeless wisdom of the game as a road map to living a fuller, happier life.

Golf is fraught with metaphors for life's travails. Each chapter of this book is organized around a particular theme that uses a historical golf reference to illustrate a particular life lesson, then concludes with practical advice on how to incorporate these lessons into your own life.

The Front Nine

"There is not a single hole that can't be birdied if you just think. But there is not one that can't be double bogeyed if you ever stop thinking."

～ Bobby Jones

1

Having a Game Plan

ↂ

VIJAY, CHARLIE, AND ESTEBAN

Forging a plan to get from where we are to where we want to go can feel like a journey of a million miles. Sometimes it helps to see the path trod by others to help us see the possibilities on our own horizons. Take for example, the varied journeys of Vijay Singh, Charlie Sifford, and Esteban Toledo to reach golfing success.

Vijay Singh knew from a very early age that he wanted to be a professional golfer. But growing up in Fiji with five siblings and his parents in a cramped little house, the world of professional golf must have seemed like a very unlikely prospect. Unlikely, that is, if you were not Vijay Singh.

As a boy, Singh loved the game so much that he would sometimes make his way through various drainage pipes that ran beneath the runways of the Nadi Airport to reach the golf course. The pipes were completely dark, and the lanky Singh had to crouch down simply to fit. The putrid water drained sewage to the ocean, and it would normally run higher than his ankles. Singh was so committed to his plan that he would drop out of school by the time he was sixteen in order to pursue his dream.

Vijay Singh was blessed with a gift and a conviction—and these would be the ticket to his dreams. His gift was his ability to play "with peace." Part of this gift was just his natural dispo-

"*If your talents are mental, you are not at a disadvantage against the physically talented person. You can plan and prepare better than he can, you can outthink him during the contest, and you can manage your game better.*"

↬ Gary Player, from
*The Golfer's Guide
to the Meaning
of Life*

sition. He had the ability to stand over a putt that might mean the difference between playing on the weekend or going home, and he would not be overcome with crushing anxiety. Vijay has long been a student of Eastern philosophy, and he has mastered the ability to control his breathing, and, as a result, his temperament in high-stress situations. Singh was also convinced from very early in his life that nothing can beat unrelenting hard work and practice. He has worn this philosophy like a shield for his entire professional career. Singh has said that the reason he has become successful is that he has always had a disposition to do "whatever it takes."

Like Singh, Charlie Sifford had to wade through plenty of filth to play golf, but the indignity he endured poured from the hearts and minds of ignorant people. Today Charlie Sifford, now in his eighties, seems relaxed and unassuming, yet his pleasant demeanor belies the trials he had to endure to realize his dream of playing professional golf against the best in the world.

Sifford is an African American, and during his prime years of playing golf, black golfers were banned from playing on the PGA Tour. Sifford would sharpen his game wherever he could. He won the National Negro Open five times straight from 1952 to 1956. Sifford has said he believed that if he kept working on his game, eventually the doors of opportunity would crack open.

Sifford made history in 1961 when he became the first African American allowed to compete on the PGA Tour. By that time, Sifford was forty-one years old, and his best playing days were behind him. Much like Jackie Robinson, Sifford was well aware of the significance of the path he was blazing. What's more, simply making it to the big dance was not the end of his struggles. Sifford endured insults, threats, and indignities virtually everywhere he played. An example was the time he was barred from eating with the other players in the men's grill room at a country club in Florida. Sifford was forced to eat in the caddie yard. Many of the other players knew that Sifford's treatment was wrong, and Ken Venturi led a group of players out to the caddie yard to dine with their friend.

"Who is going to be second?"

～ Walter Hagen,
    frequently spoken
    before a competition

That Sifford could remain focused and committed to his plan to become a professional golfer is an incredible testament to his fortitude. Sifford would go on to win the 1967 Hartford Open and the 1969 L.A. Open. He won the latter in a play-off over Harold Henning at nearly fifty years old.

It is commonplace that great golfers are measured by the number of major tournaments they have won. But Charlie Sifford's victory over racial injustice could be the greatest success story the game has ever known.

Esteban Toledo also had to overcome great odds to make it as a professional golfer along a path that was marked by extreme poverty, death, and a fighting spirit.

Toledo was born in Mexicali, Mexico as the youngest of eleven children. The family lived in a "choza," the Mexican word for a hut. Actually, "hut" as a description of his family's living conditions probably paints too nice a picture. The reality of their existence in the barrio was near destitution. Their tiny house had no plumbing, and their roof leaked like a river during even the smallest amount of rain, probably due to the fact that their roof was little more than cardboard. His family was forced to find space for all of them to sleep on two small beds.

Life was hard on Toledo and his family. When he was a small boy his older brother was found dead in a river, probably murdered. The thought that by 1994 Toledo would be playing on the PGA Tour was inconceivable.

But Toledo was a fighter, literally. Searching for a way to break out of gripping poverty, Toledo turned his hopes toward becoming a boxer. He fought with a ferocity that allowed him to amass a 12–1 professional record. His boxing took him to Tijuana, Los Angeles, and Las Vegas. He was once paid $5,000 for a fight in Las Vegas. Toledo thought boxing would be his ticket to freedom, but reality once again put him down for the count.

An infection set in after appendicitis surgery and his boxing days were done. So it was back to the barrio for Toledo. He landed a job at a dusty golf course on the border—the same course where as a kid he used to sell golf balls he found back to the golfers for three for a dollar. Now he was cleaning clubs, shining shoes, doing whatever the boss told him to do. In the small slivers of time when he was not working, he would swing a golf club until the boss told him to stop.

One day, Toledo met Jon Minnis. Minnis was from California, but he might as well have been from heaven. Minnis was kindhearted, and he saw potential in Toledo. Minnis took Toledo under his wing and brought him back to California, away from the oppression of the barrio. Minnis found him a place to live and helped him to become a golfer, nurturing Toledo's natural athleticism into a highly proficient yet simple swing. Toledo calls Minnis his father for the kindness and mentoring he has provided.

To this day, Toledo's boxing instincts continue to serve him on the golf course. Toledo believes that boxing teaches you patience under pressure—the pressure of someone trying to knock you out. Toledo learned that the game of golf is like boxing in that you have to wait for your chances. You need to be patient until opportunity presents itself, but while you are waiting you need to work and be prepared. Clearly, Toledo knows the value of hard work and preparation, and he has been smart enough to turn opportunity into success.

The varied paths of Singh, Sifford, and Toledo prove that with conviction and tenacity a dream can be turned into reality.

~~~

Having a Game Plan

In the 1926 Walker Cup matches, Bobby Jones faced Cyril Tolley in a critical match. Tolley was a large, strapping man who prided himself on his prodigious drives. Jones, ever the thinking man's golfer, knew that all he had to do to throw Tolley off his game was to out-drive him. On his first drive, Jones gave his swing a bit more effort, resulting in a drive that finished almost ten yards past Tolley's. That was enough to cause Tolley to completely abandon any game plan he had come into the match with, and he spent the day slashing away at the ball with massive swings in a vain attempt to protect his self-image. Jones went on to win not only the psychological match but the formal contest as well, by 12 and 11 in the thirty-six-hole match.

Bobby Jones' mental strategy illustrates that without a crystal clear idea of who you are and where you feel your strengths are, then under the burning heat of competition even the most talented can go astray. Great champions use a particular aspect of personality or technique as an emotional anchor during times of high pressure. Gary Player, competing against the likes of Nicklaus and Palmer, then Trevino, Miller, and Watson among others, used his peak physical conditioning as a basis of mental strength. He did not necessarily measure his capacity to compete against these titans by the position of their drives, for if he had, his competitive psyche would have taken a constant beating. Instead, he concentrated on the fact that his physical conditioning would enable him to maintain an edge on his competition over the course of a long and grueling tournament. His game plan was to literally outlast them.

Paul Runyan was another player who decided that he would fortify himself with the development of an aspect of his game that

"The old trite saying of 'one shot at a time'?
It was not trite to me. I live it."

ꕔ Mickey Wright

offset his deficiencies. Runyan would routinely give up yardage, sometimes fifty yards or more, against the likes of Sam Snead. Yet Runyan, perhaps one of the most physically disciplined golfers of all time (along with Player), developed a short game that was so lethal that he came to be known as "Little Poison" for his capacity to break your heart around the greens.

These examples illustrate the thirst most golfers have for more distance and how this desire can sometimes work against them. So great is this insatiable desire for the magic elixir of a 300-yard drive that many competitors find their mental strength broken on the first few holes of a match simply due to the fact that they are being out-driven. While this certainly is a problem for the distance-challenged, it more often than not affects golfers who believe they possess great distance only to be humbled by a (usually younger) more limber opponent. A few overswung attempts that end up sliced into the rough or hooked out of bounds prove that chasing a longer opponent off the tee only ends up in crushing defeat both in the competition and for your ego. Jones played this strategy to perfection against Tolley.

Professional golfers need to maintain mental road maps of what they wish to accomplish in a tournament, season, or career. They need to know what aspects of their games they can most count on when the pressure is on, and they need to be honest about where the weaknesses are in their games so that they can work to minimize them. They also need to set goals to measure success or failure in these areas.

On the golf course or off we all need a clear picture of what our game plans are. Where is it that we want to end up? How do we get there?

Often, people have a vague idea of what their ideal goal or destination is, such as "I want to be rich," or even "I want to be on the Tour." Unfortunately, most of us have no game plan, or map for getting there. How do you know where you will end up when you have no route to get there?

Jack Canfield, cocreator of the phenomenally successful book

"Match your strategy to your skills."

~ Arnold Palmer

series *Chicken Soup for the Soul*, recently released his book *The Success Principles* (HarperCollins, 2005). In it, Jack recommends that we get as detailed an understanding and description as possible about what we want our goals to be. Right down to the exact date we will achieve these things, such as graduate with an advanced degree, move into the dream house, or break 70 (or 80 or 90). This way, we actually convince our minds to train our thinking that we are well on the way to achieving all that we strive for and to draw us to the resources and circumstances that will help us achieve our goals.

We all need to sharpen our game plans. We all need to craft a specific plan that will help us achieve *specific* goals. Then, we need to concentrate our time, energy, and efforts with laserlike precision on achieving our goals. It is critically important to write them down. I like an approach that embodies short-term, intermediate, and long-term goals. Short-term goals should be worked on every day, intermediate during the course of a season, and long-term at least twice a year (particularly at the end of the year). These become the mile markers against which we can measure our progress and gauge the distance left to achieve our current goals and then to establish new ones.

Once you have a game plan, in golf or in life, it serves as an internal compass to keep you on the path to achieving anything you want regardless of what the competition throws at you.

"Golf is usually played with the outward appearance of great dignity. It is, nevertheless, a game of considerable passion, either of the explosive type or that which burns inwardly."

~ Bobby Jones

2

Unstoppable Passion

༄

SLEEPING ON IT

How far would you go to pursue your dreams?

Would you leave behind everything you have ever known, including family, friends, security, and even the country you have lived in all your life?

Would you be willing to give up all of this, travel thousands of miles, and then exist in the basest conditions just for the chance of grasping your goals?

PGA Tour golfer Mark Hensby did just that.

The year was 1994 when a twenty-two-year-old Hensby set out to discover his destiny in America. He left his tiny hometown of Tamworth, Australia with the crazy idea that he would make it big on golf's biggest stage, the PGA Tour. He came prepared to finance his grand plan with a total of $2,000 to his name.

Friends, relatives, and coaches back home in Australia remember Hensby as a man that was more than determined—he was obsessed. They described the young pro-want-to-be as "a bit wild," "a fiery little bugger," "with a bit of a chip on his shoulders," and in need of "a psychologist more than a golf coach." And these were the people closest to him!

Hensby's bankroll took an immediate hit when he purchased an old Ford hatchback to help cart around his clubs and his aspi-

*"When it comes to the game of life, I figure
I've played the whole course."*

❧ Lee Trevino

rations. Hensby was soon to find out that the old Ford clunker was to play a much more dramatic role in his search for fame and fortune.

Hensby settled in suburban Chicago with a friend he knew from home. However, soon after his arrival, his friend was transferred, and Hensby was left out in the cold, quite literally. Having no other place to stay, Hensby took up residence for six weeks in the old Ford in the parking lot at Cog Hill Golf and Country Club, where he practiced when he wasn't caddieing at nearby Butler National Golf Club. Unfortunately for Hensby, his odyssey happened to take place in the late fall, and anyone who knows anything about Chicago knows just how cold it can be in October and November.

"You wake up, turn the heater on, and drive around the parking lot a few times. The car would feel warm for about an hour. I'd do that a few times a night," was the way Hensby would later describe his nightly warming ritual.

Hensby had another problem to deal with as well. His visa had expired. Hensby had a ticket to get back home to Australia, yet the ticket was for December 20, and he did not have the funds to pay for a change in itinerary. So, he did what he had to do. He laid low and tried to stay warm in a world that must have seemed particularly cold.

There can be no doubt that Hensby had his moments of shivering doubt, times of inner reflection when he must have wondered if all of this was worth the restless pursuit of a dream. Yet, as is often the case with true passion, Hensby's dream had as much a grip on him as he had on it. "If you're going to do something, you're going to do whatever it takes," he said.

About three weeks before he was due to fly home, his nocturnal den on wheels was discovered by the rangemaster, who spotted him one early morning. Luckily, his plight was met with compassion, and the man helped him find a place to stay until he went home for the holidays.

After Hensby received his mother's verbal lashing for his

near-destitute existence, his older brother Darren loaned him $5,000 to go back to the United States and continue the pursuit of his dreams. He put his brother's money and faith to good use, attending the 1995 PGA Tour qualifying school and turning professional.

Ten years later, in the 2004 season, Hensby won $2.7 million on the PGA Tour.

As for the old Ford, Hensby harbors no sentimentality about his temporary shelter. He has said that he figures he sold the car for a net of about $100 (after having to buy new tires). Today, Hensby drives a Mercedes.

Certainly, it is safe to assume that Mark Hensby is sleeping much more soundly these days, knowing that dreams are more than what we do with our eyes closed—they are something to be passionately pursued, no matter what it takes.

~~

Unstoppable Passion

Golfers hoping to secure a tee time at the formidable Black Course at Bethpage, site of the 2002 U.S. Open won by Tiger Woods, will stop at nothing for a chance to play the legendary track. It is not the least bit unusual for a golfer, coming off a grueling week at work, to pull an all-nighter in the parking lot at Bethpage waiting for one of the relatively few and coveted Saturday morning tee times on one of the nation's top public golf masterpieces.

What possibly could motivate individuals who can hardly drag themselves off of the couch when their spouses ask them to take out the garbage to endure such inconvenience and hardship just to play a weekly round of golf? The answer, of course, is simple. It is passion.

Passion is an unstoppable force. Passion is not something that is given to us. It is always there, but it sometimes requires that we discover it. Other times we know exactly where passion lies; we just choose to ignore it. But passion is unrelenting, and refusing to pursue it will not make it go away but will only make us feel frustrated and unfulfilled.

I believe that the most powerful forces in the universe are faith, love, and passion. They are the foundations upon which a happy, productive, and purposeful life is based. We all possess an infinite capacity for each. The key to fulfilling our passion is to identify it, commit to follow it, and nurture its possibilities.

Identifying our passion is not always easy. Oftentimes it is buried under layers of self-limiting images of what we are capable of. These layers are built up over time by the societal forces around us that attempt to keep everyone on a level playing field,

"Visualize winning."

↝ Gary Player

well below our individual and collective abilities. It is based upon the notion that success and achievement are reserved for a privileged few who have been born with certain talents. The reality is that champions are never born, they are made. Those who succeed do so because they have made a choice to be winners—to rise above the din of doubt and reject any option except to see their dreams realized by employing the power of their passion.

Many people find it difficult to discover their passion. I think a good way to discover our passion is to make note of the things we know we are *not* passionate about. Systematically crossing off that for which we have no passion will eventually lead us to the things that we do embrace. Sometimes it helps to keep a journal of your discoveries in this regard.

Committing to following your passion entails a *100 percent personal commitment*. I like to approach *100 percent personal commitments* from the standpoint of a personal contract. Write your commitment down in great detail; commit to completion dates of each aspect; date it and sign it. Review it at least once a week. Hold yourself to the contract.

Nurturing your passion is critical, for it will provide you with the roadmap to reach your goals. One of the best ways to do this is to practice *dream building*. Allow yourself to fantasize what it would be like to be living the life you are passionate about. What would your relationships with your spouse, loved ones, and friends be like? What kind of career would you have, and how would your peers and coworkers treat you? How much money would you make, where would you live, and what kind of car would you drive?

Perhaps your passion would be fulfilled if you were a PGA Tour professional? What kind of Tour pro would you be? What kind of clothing would you wear, what endorsement would you have, and what kind of equipment would you use? How would you treat your fellow pros, the fans, and the media? What aspects of your game would define you?

Experts confirm that most successful people have always had

"Always keep learning. It keeps you young."

~ Patty Berg

some sense that they would accomplish extraordinary things. Even before he was a blip on the international golf landscape, a young golfer named Arnold Palmer used to practice his autograph for the day when there would be more fans who would want it than he had ink in a pen. Perhaps you should get ready for your stardom as a hugely successful Tour player, business tycoon, inspiring teacher, caring social worker, or loving parent by practicing a few autographs!

An enjoyable aspect of my career is the regular opportunity I have to speak before groups of high school and college students. Students of that age are great audiences because they are so full of positive energy. They have a mindset that nothing can stop them. They embrace their boundless potential.

One of the more endearing aspects of this audience is the variety of "types" I see as I look out. The students allow themselves to be whatever image they have of themselves. They literally live the image as though they have already accomplished it—and, as we know from marketing, image becomes reality. I look out on the crowd, and I see movie stars, rock and rap artists, journalists, technology experts, world-famous athletes, directors, entrepreneurs, and many, many more. I love the liberty students give themselves to live their dreams. Their passion has not yet been beaten down by a culture of resignation that tries to constantly divorce us from our dreams. Of course, there are grounds for a word of caution to these groups where I emphasize that they cannot allow the image of success to cloud the fundamental steps to achieving it through a solid education and hard work.

We all need to maintain a youthful passion for what we do and who we are (or who we are meant to be). One of the first areas of self-analysis relates to our careers. Do we love what we are doing? The best way to test this is to ask ourselves if we would continue to do our current job if we had to do it for free? How many of us love our jobs so much that if they no longer netted any monetary return we would do them anyway, just out of fulfillment and joy? A clear example of many golfers' passion for the game is you will often hear people proclaim that they would do any job

"If you want to keep the fire of your passion burning, you need to make sure it has plenty of fuel."

in golf "for free" just to be near the game. If we are not ready to do our jobs for free, then we need to do some serious thinking about what is missing.

Taking steps to nurture your passion includes taking classes, lessons, reading, finding clubs and support groups, and getting a part-time job in a field that you have an interest in. Seek out others who have made it in the field you desire to work in, and ask them how they did it.

Also, just as a professional golfer keeps constant tabs on his or her swing, be sure to keep a close watch on your enthusiasm. If you want to keep the fire of your passion burning, you need to make sure it has plenty of fuel. All of the steps outlined in this chapter, including dream building and taking concrete steps like additional education, will help to keep you on plane if you practice them regularly.

Just like the golfers who huddle through the cold night in the hope of securing a tee time, following your passion can carry you through the most obstinate obstacles.

"When you lose your temper after missing a shot, the chances are you will miss the next shot, too."

～ Julius Boros

3

Proactive vs. Reactive

་ཟ

GRABBING A GATOR BY THE TAIL

Sometimes there is no time to think. No time to weigh the pros and cons. No luxury of logic to guide your course of action. You simply react.

Such was the case for journeyman PGA Tour professional Ken Green one sunny September day in 2004 when a pleasant game of throw and fetch with his best friend Nip, a two-year-old German shepherd, would turn into a struggle of life and death.

Green is a man who has lived both sides of success. He is a five-time Tour winner who has known the trappings of celebrity, power, money, and entitlement. Johnny Miller once called him the best fairway wood player in the game. At the height of his fame in the late eighties Green would commonly be the first choice, over names like Norman, Floyd, and Crenshaw, of the rich and powerful when they had the first pick in pre-tournament pro-am draw parties. Green was the perfect host. His humble Danbury, Connecticut origins, his killer instincts on the golf course, and his tendency for being eccentric (remember the green shoes?) made him fun to be around, if only because you never really knew what he would do next.

Green was smart enough to take advantage of the worldwide stage upon which he was performing and naïve enough to think that the good times would last forever. Then, life happened.

"If you prepare for months and months and set high goals, the last thing to do is be in my own way. There's two people in me; one calm and one totally excited. The calm one won today."

ॐ Annika Sorenstam

Divorce, injuries, uncertainty, and finally depression all took their toll.

But Ken Green is a fighter, and he was determined to strike back against long odds. It is probably a good thing that Green possessed such a disposition, or at least it was for a hyper dog named Nip.

Enjoying a simple game of catch in the backyard on a nice day with Nip was something Green had done countless times before. In fact, Nip was more than a house dog that would become reacquainted with her master every four or five weeks when he was off the road from one Tour stop or another. Rather, Nip was a road warrior. A constant sidekick, a ride-along-in-the-RV companion. The two were inseparable.

A professional athlete of Green's caliber possesses exceptional hand-eye coordination, yet a slightly off-line toss to Nip and the dog's overexuberant early leap nudged the ball over a fence and into a murky canal. Canals of this sort are commonplace in Florida, and the locals typically leave them alone lest they disturb any number of natural inhabitants that populated the region long before the likes of Ken Green. Among these natives are alligators.

Nip did what Nip does, and she bounded into the thick water to retrieve the ball. Only after Nip's initial splash, Green heard a second splash that struck a primal nerve. Green's worst fears were confirmed when he saw an alligator of an estimated seven feet gliding toward Nip in preparation for attack. His mind raced as it tried to sort through how to react and save his best friend. However, his course of action was decided for him when he heard the dog yelp and get pulled under in the jaws of the prehistoric predator. Green bounded into the water up to his neck without any real plan other than to do whatever he could to save Nip. At first, there was nothing as dog and alligator were both submerged. Then the alligator's tail waved directly in front of him, and Green grabbed it and started pulling it toward him, as in a roadside alligator-wrestling match of decades past. But this contest was on the alligator's turf. Green allowed his knees to

"An Open [Championship] is not really only a measure of how you handle a golf course, it is a measure of how you handle yourself, how patient you are, how experienced you are."

~ Jack Nicklaus

buckle and used his body weight to fall backward, now completely submerged, still grasping the huge reptile. After a few moments of Green's incessant tugging, the surprised alligator released his grip on Nip. If Green was pleased that his dog had been released, he also knew that in the next few minutes he might well be sacrificing his own life for Nip's—the alligator surely could turn his massive power onto the attacking Green in self-protection, if nothing else. Luckily, the alligator simply swam away, perhaps deciding that anything, or anyone, that would be crazy enough to grab it by the tail in five feet of muddy water was best not to mess with. Green and Nip swam ashore, where Nip needed twenty-five stitches in her front left leg and shoulder and Green would nurse bruised ribs from the gator's powerful tail.

One has to wonder whether Green will now view his competitors a little differently on the golf course, for how tough can they really be compared to his tangle with an alligator?

At the very least the incident proves the value, or stupidity, depending upon your perspective, of not thinking, but just reacting.

"Golf is like driving a car. As you get older, you get more careful."

~ Sam Snead

~⁊~

Proactors vs. Reactors

The game of golf has a way of divulging aspects of our character that we would probably prefer were left hidden, sometimes even from ourselves.

Most golfers fall into one of two categories: Proactors or Reactors.

Reactors answer events with a hair-trigger response. It is usually fueled by anger, fear, or both. It follows an event immediately and without due consideration of consequence.

Proactors react in a measured and logical manner. They engage their full faculties prior to taking action. They have a plan, both to bring about success and to diminish the consequences if they fail.

Having personality characteristics of a Reactor is not without some merits, yet these traits are better reserved for matters of life or death when any delay in action can result in dire consequences. Being, or becoming, a Proactor has benefits that will enhance every aspect of your life.

On the golf course it is easy to spot Reactors (it is ironic that nuclear plants are referred to as "reactors") versus Proactors. Reactors are usually flashy, capable of creating great excitement, and, on any given day, setting the course record. But for those who know them, it is just a matter of time until the slightest adversity causes them to overheat. Often times the response is so involuntary that it provides a glimpse into a person's true character, as a river of expletives, accusations, and club throwing defines a river of rage.

Meanwhile, the Proactors continue to stick to their game plan. They take advantage of opportunity when they can, and

"I expect to hit at least five bad shots."

～ Walter Hagen, on
expecting adversity

they accept adversity as a common, and expected, part of the process.

It is not a surprise, then, that golfers like Hogan and Nicklaus, two of the all-time best Proactors, have collected an inordinate amount of trophies.

Acknowledging which camp we fall into is the first step to exploiting the advantage if we are already Proactors or modifying our negative behavior if we are Reactors.

A good way to come to recognize your true nature in this regard is to monitor your daily driving habits (I am referring to driving your car, not golf balls for this example). When you get behind the wheel, do you feel that it is "you against the world?" When one of your fellow motorists does something foolish, reckless, or downright dangerous, do you feel personally attacked and compelled to "get even"? Do you view a drive on the highway as a method of getting from point A to point B, or is it a race that you must win?

We all likely possess some degree of the above emotions, and many mistakenly point to such behavior as examples of their competitive and aggressive natures. Raw, uncontrolled, aggressive behavior, even when we feel like we have been victims is dangerous. A proactive response takes into account consequences and maintains the perspective that being a successful road warrior is no more productive than ripping another drive on the same line as the one that just dove into the lake, just to prove you can do it, to get even.

Even Bobby Jones was known to have a hot temper on the golf course in his youth, but he learned to control it, to become proactive and less reactive.

We all have the ability to modify our thinking and behavior, and the change will not only improve performance, but also help us to enjoy the ride.

"Through preparation and hard work, you can prepare yourself for a mental attitude, a zone. When it happens, all you see is the ball and the hole."

↣ Payne Stewart

4

Visualizing Success

৵

A VISIONARY SEASON

One of the more remarkable years in professional golf was the one notched by Jack Nicklaus in 1972. Individual athletic performances aside, his accomplishments in that year were as much an example of vision as of execution.

Jack Nicklaus lost his father, Charlie, to cancer in 1970 at the age of only fifty-six. This, coupled with the 1971 death of his idol, Bobby Jones, from complications of a spinal disease, caused Nicklaus to reassess his career and recommit himself to the game. Nicklaus decided that he would attempt to scale the immortal path blazed by Jones in winning his era's Grand Slam, by becoming the first man to win all four of the professional Majors in one year.

Nicklaus began his march at the Masters. He led all four rounds and posted a three-stroke victory at Augusta, finishing at two under, as the only player to break par. While a three-stroke victory would suggest a typically Nicklaus-like dominating performance, the great golfer was actually uncharacteristically shaky down the back nine stretch on Sunday. Fortunately for him, so was his competition, and none could mount a charge.

Perhaps his jitters occurred because he was chasing history, his aspirations, and golfing immortality. Or perhaps they came

"Ask yourself how many shots you would have saved if you never lost your temper, never got down on yourself, always developed a strategy before you hit, and always played within your capabilities."

↜ Jack Nicklaus

from the pressure of doing exactly what everyone expected him to do, for Nicklaus was far and away the pre-tournament favorite.

Regardless of how he accomplished it, with his victory at the Masters he would tie Arnold Palmer with four Green Jackets, jump past Walter Hagen on the all-time list of Majors won, and stand only one Major victory away from his hero, Bobby Jones, who had won thirteen Majors (including his U.S. and British Amateur titles).

If the weight of history lay heavily upon Nicklaus' shoulders, then it was surely blown from its perch by the final round of the windy 1972 U.S. Open at Pebble Beach.

Nicklaus entered the final round with a one-shot lead over Lee Trevino, two shots ahead of Kermit Zarley and Bruce Crampton, and three in front of Arnold Palmer. Palmer would take a run at Nicklaus and close the gap to just one shot by the twelfth hole. But, by the time Nicklaus reached the seventeenth tee, he had worked his lead back up to three strokes. He then proceeded to hit one of his most famous shots. Playing into a stiff breeze, Nicklaus struck his ball with his 1-iron with such accuracy that the ball actually hit the pin and settled some five inches from it. The birdie insured what would end as a three-stroke victory over a surging Bruce Crampton.

The next stage of Nicklaus' quest would be the Open Championship at Muirfield.

Nicklaus prepared for this major with the same intense preparation as he had all others. He arrived early and checked into the Greywalls Hotel, which overlooks the tenth tee, for practice and to get acclimated. Nicklaus loved Muirfield, having competed there successfully as a Walker Cup member in 1959 and winning the Open Championship there in 1966.

It is a matter of record that through the first two rounds of the tournament, Nicklaus trailed Lee Trevino and Tony Jacklin by one stroke. What is not widely known is that Nicklaus had been suffering all week with a sore neck that inhibited his ability to swing freely. This condition, coupled with a conservative game plan on a course that can get you into trouble quickly, caused Nicklaus to drop six shots behind the leader Trevino and five shots behind Jacklin after three rounds. In fact, Trevino finished his round with a flourish, making birdies at five consecutive holes and posting a 66 to Nicklaus' 71.

Nicklaus awoke on the morning of the final round free of pain and convinced he should be aggressive, feeling that if he could post a score of 65, it should be enough to win. Nicklaus would go out in 32, including a birdie on the ninth hole. He would continue the streak on the tenth, and when he also birdied the eleventh hole, he was in sole possession of the lead. Meanwhile, behind him, Trevino and Jacklin started to mount a counterattack, with each scoring an eagle on the ninth. Nicklaus was well aware that neither player was likely to fold, so he would have to finish strong. Fate stepped in when he missed an eight-foot birdie putt at the fifteenth hole that witnesses reported seemed to be kept out of the hole by air alone. At this point, he felt he would need to go one under over the last three holes. However, Nicklaus would bogey the sixteenth hole, his first bogey of the day, and par the seventeenth and eighteenth holes, finishing two strokes higher over the final holes than where he thought he needed to be. He would post a final-round score of 66. Nicklaus' Grand Slam hopes were now in the hands of the two men behind him.

Both Trevino and Jacklin were tied at six under as they came to the pivotal par-5, seventeenth hole. Trevino proceeded to hit four uncharacteristically poor shots, and as he approached his ball in the rough, past the pin, he seemed to have given up the fight. Trevino quickly swatted at the ball in an effort he would later admit was "a give-up chip." Remarkably, the chip shot went into the hole to preserve par. An understandably rattled Jacklin three-putted the hole for bogey. Trevino took full advantage of his new lease on life by securing a solid par at the eighteenth hole to secure the championship and deny Nicklaus golf's first professional Grand Slam.

Even though Jack Nicklaus did not win the Grand Slam, the mere fact that he had the vision to attempt it and the talent to nearly accomplish it attests that he deserves his lofty profile among the game's greatest players.

"Management, placing the ball in the right position for the next shot, is eighty percent of winning golf."

᭜ Ben Hogan

~

Visualizing Success

A friend of mine recently confided in me that in his mind he has played nearly all of the great courses in the world. Between books, the Golf Channel, and the Internet, he can quote the yardage, architect, topography, and an endless series of other minutiae pertaining to courses from Augusta National and Pebble Beach to the Old Course at St. Andrews and scores of others.

"What do you feel like when you are on these courses?" I asked.

"I feel everything. I feel the breeze from the Georgia pines at Augusta National; I feel the mist in my face at Pebble Beach. I feel a hard North Sea wind at the Old Course. Although it is only in my mind, I am never more alive than on these magical courses. They are God's gardens. The colors, they are so vibrant, and the smell of the fresh cut grass is like a sweet perfume. Everything is perfect. Just like heaven on earth," he mused.

"What do you shoot on these courses?"

At that point, my friend's gaze fixed itself on the dancing flames in the fireplace, and it was clear that this question had thrown him into a deep, pensive reverie. After a few minutes, he slowly turned his head toward mine and gazed at me with a bewildered, faraway look, declaring, "Matt, I've never even considered it. The thought of doing anything more on these courses than simply swimming in the joy of the time and place has never even crossed my mind. Since it is all a fantasy, I suppose the next time I take my mental journey I might as well keep score, eh?"

"What do you think your score will be then?"

"Oh, you know me, I will be lucky to break ninety."

My friend's golf holiday around the globe is not unique. We all fantasize about things we would love to experience. It is also common that we limit our dreams to fit our self-image. Isn't it remarkable that while we can use our minds to create anything we want, we allow ourselves to be self-limiting even in the limitless universe of our minds?

Visualization, with purpose, can be the most powerful tool in the world to achieve your goals and objectives.

Study after study has concluded that planting a detailed image in your subconscious mind can actually trick your mind into thinking that the image is real. It is a process that has been used by some of the most prominent people in all of history, including Albert Einstein, and countless successful leaders and business executives. Ben Hogan and Jack Nicklaus were two of the more prominent golfers who utilized the technique. Nicklaus has said, "I never hit a shot, not even in practice, without having a very sharp, in-focus picture of it in my head. It's like a color movie." It is safe to assume that Nicklaus' *movies* were all Oscar-worthy.

Many modern mental coaches encourage visualization as a method to achieve success whether your goal is to play better golf, become your company's top salesperson, or anything else. The key is that when you visualize, you need to insure that your mental image is as vivid and detailed as possible. My friend did a good job at that aspect of visualization, but it is critically important that your visualization is done with a specific intent if you wish to use it to reach your goals. See yourself hitting perfect drives, approach shots, pitches, chips, and putts. Do not be afraid to let your ball get swept up in a gale and pushed into a bunker. But see yourself hitting a perfect bunker shot to save par, or maybe even sneak in a birdie. See yourself as if you are watching yourself on a movie screen. Everything about you, including your swing, is perfect. You are the ideal image of yourself. Put yourself in situations that would normally raise your level of anxiety. Maybe you are teeing off the first tee in front of your weekly league, where heckling has been risen to an art form. Maybe it is your first round of golf with your father-in-law at his club, or you are playing with the boss or your chief golfing adversary. Put yourself in the most trying situations you can image and then see yourself succeed again and again and again, for it is in the constant, positive repetition that the mind begins to accept this *reality rehearsal* as the real thing. Do this visualization exercise as often as possible, and try to do it when you are the most relaxed and not distracted.

How do you envision yourself when you fantasize a round in your mind? What is the flight of your golf ball? Is it a weak slice, or is it a powerful, long, soaring drive? How do you envision yourself in your inner mind's eye in other stressful situations? How do you see yourself when you want to ask your boss for a raise or ask a difficult customer to place a large order? Are these situations so discomforting that you do not even want to consider them in your visualization, when you can easily craft the image however you choose? Do you allow yourself to be a champion or to slink away in defeat?

Visualization is your chance not only to play the greatest courses of your life but to shoot your personal best. Visualization proves that if you can think it, then you can do it.

"I started golf at eight. Dad had an auto body repair shop. He and mom sacrificed all the time. Every extra cent was used to get me into amateur tournaments. They gave up things to make sure I had clothes that looked nice. They would go without, so I could have three new balls or new socks. My wonderful parents gave me the opportunity to compete with the best and get the experience I needed to be successful."

∿ Nancy Lopez

5

Finding the Time

ॐ

Somewhere, likely buried in the ever-shifting sand traps of the Iraqi desert, is a trail of golf balls.

The trail marks the path that the 426th Forward Support Battalion took as it pushed from Kuwait into Northern Iraq during the early stages of the war. The dimple-dotted line ends in Mosul, where one man's passion for golf continues to change the lives of those around him.

In March 2003 1st Lt. Jesse White, a shop officer for the U.S. Army's elite 101st Airborne division, was on the verge of putting into practice that for which he had trained most of his professional life.

His departure from Fort Campbell, Kentucky, in early support of the war in Iraq was planned, and his supplies were well tended.

Chemical suit, gas mask, flak jacket, rifle, ammunition, and a must for the deserts of Iraq—a sand wedge.

---

*This wonderful story was penned by Mark Cubbedge, Manager of Communications at the World Golf Hall of Fame in St. Augustine, Florida. Mark is a golf historian and published author. Obviously, his passion for the game and love for his country burn brightly. This piece was originally written in November of 2003.

"In addition to preparing the mind, you must prepare the muscles for a round of golf. The average golfer claims he hasn't the time to warm up, when the truth is he won't make or take the time. A four-hour round of golf can certainly be preceded by ten or fifteen minutes on the practice tee. By simply hitting a dozen balls you have eliminated three or four bad holes from your system. If you won't hit practice shots, at least swing something heavy before driving off."

꙳ Jackie Burke Jr.

White didn't know exactly what awaited him in places far less friendly than his home in White House, Tennessee, a city of just over three thousand households, though he had heard the stories of camel spiders, scorpions, snakes, and opportunistic insurgents.

The one thing White did know was that he needed to find room for that wedge, along with his 7-iron, 4-wood, and a few hundred used golf balls. He knew swatting around some x-outs would likely be one of the few distractions that could bring a feeling of home to such a distant and dangerous place.

As White and the rest of the battalion crossed from Kuwait into Iraq bound for Mosul, White made the most of his free time during stops. White, who maintains a 4 handicap, and some of his fellow soldiers would fire off a few swings into the vastness of the desert.

Stops in places like An Najaf and Al Hillah were nothing like life in the Volunteer State or Fort Campbell, but it mattered little. Thoughts often drifted to Raymond Floyd's Legacy Golf Course in Springfield, Tennessee, or Fort Campbell's Cole Park Golf Course, which were visited weekly by White before he headed overseas.

"Me and some of the guys in my unit would hit a few at some of our various stops," White recalled in 2005. "Nothing crazy, just a few to restore a sense of normalcy to it all—if you can call hitting golf balls into the desert of Iraq normal."

By late May the 426th Forward Support Battalion had reached their semi-permanent home of Qayyarah West Airfield near Mosul, and White was determined to keep golf as part of his weekly routine.

So he set out to create what is widely believed to be Iraq's first golf course—albeit, one far from a plush country club setting.

White's creation—dubbed the TPC at Mosul in honor of some of the finest courses played on the PGA Tour—had features that included rocks, ammo, old aircraft parts, and concertina wire.

As one of White's fellow soldiers put it: "Our fairways have real bunkers in them."

"I finally found the guy I used to know on the golf course. It was me."

       ⌇ Jack Nicklaus, after
           winning the 1986
           Masters

White methodically carved out his desert course with all the free time he was afforded during a war. His passion pushed him, and he received encouragement along the way from battalion commander Lt. Col. Jeff Kelley, who was nearly as addicted to the game as was White.

White managed to pick up a shovel and dig through waist-high piles of dirt as he carved out the first hole, a 130-yard par 3, which essentially was a one-lane driving range. The green, not empty of tank tracks, was marked by an old radio antenna stuck into the ground with a shop rag tied around the end. The teeing area was marked by a pair of bomb fins.

With Kelley's blessing White dedicated any spare moments outside of his military obligations. White's duties—assigning repairs for broken vehicles, weapons, and communications systems in a mechanical environment where sand is nearly as uncooperative as the insurgents—made for extremely long days. They were made a bit longer as White pursued his desert design.

Two more par 3s eventually took shape, the second measuring 40 yards and the third 110. Another month later White added three more holes, two par 4s of about 250 yards apiece and a par 3 of 140 yards. White, who single-handedly served as architect, grounds crew, and player, built the final tee box on an earth-covered bunker so players would have to take the elevation into consideration.

Most of the soldiers initially thought White was crazy. It didn't take them long, however, to realize he was the one most likely to keep his sanity, as he worked in nine holes every Saturday with Kelley, Maj. Spencer Smith, and Maj. Kirk Whitson.

The course's first hole, located next to the main maintenance facility, had a way of enticing soldiers to step between the two bomb fins and leave reality behind for a few minutes.

In all more than a hundred soldiers took up a club, and roughly four foursomes could be seen playing a round during any given week.

"The course, at times, was our only source of solace," White said in 2005. "It was probably the most enjoyable ninety minutes of our week."

As word of White's creation made it back to the United States, the PGA Tour adopted White's battalion and supported his efforts. The Tour sent cups, flagsticks, and vast amounts of other supplies—as well as a shipment of nearly one ton of food and snacks.

"TPC at Mosul" hats and shirts followed—including one signed for White by Tour Commissioner Tim Finchem. Other golf organizations pitched in, as did other golf-loving civilians.

More than one thousand golf clubs, and that number many times over in golf balls, eventually made their way over to help the soldiers enjoy some R&R and to add to White's vision.

One of the soldiers White introduced to the game was Capt. Kate Blaise. She had never played the game, despite being married to a man who loved it. Both Kate and husband Mike were in the 101st Airborne, so time together was precious, and learning the game always awaited another day.

Under White's instruction, Blaise began to learn more and more about the game. She became a regular at the TPC at Mosul, and her swing rounded into form. Her passion seemed to grow almost daily, and as she wound up her tour in Iraq in January 2004, she said she didn't know what the future held, only that golf would be a big part of it.

Tragically, Mike would not return with Kate to play golf back in the States. On January 23 Mike lost his life when the helicopter he was piloting crashed near Mosul.

White, who was married by a pastor/teaching pro, still gets plenty of e-mails from friends he's never met—from those who sent items to him and his fellow soldiers at the TPC at Mosul to those who simply have heard his story.

In 2005 White and his family were buying a new house in White House, Tennessee. When he walked into the model home he apologized for interrupting the real estate agent, who was engrossed in reading.

She kindly put the magazine down and told White he was no interruption, apologizing for her lack of attention by trying to explain the story that had her so wrapped up.

White was taken aback as she described in detail a story about a soldier who had carved out a golf course in the deserts of Iraq.

And how this soldier had taken the time to bring a female captain under his wing and teach her the game, learning that her husband lost his life just days before returning home.

"We all still miss Mike a lot," White said.

The real estate agent was almost in shock, grabbing the magazine and returning to the first page of the article, where a photo of White stared back.

Tears began to flow from her eyes down her cheeks. A full-fledged crying session followed, before she regained her composure and had White autograph the magazine.

That magazine made its way to the real estate company's next corporate meeting, where the agent announced to everyone that a hero was moving into their new development.

"It's very humbling," White said, "and quite an honor someone gets so excited about meeting me."

Such is the trail you've blazed.

"*I don't know if you're ever finished trying to improve. As soon as you feel like you are finished, then I guess you are finished, because you already put a limit on your ability and what you can attain. I don't think that is right.*"

∽ Tiger Woods

$\curvearrowright$

Finding the Time

"Golf takes too long to play."

How often have we all heard that?

We all have more demands on our time today then ever before. Whether it's families, careers, or hobbies that push us over the edge, we just do not seem to be able to fit it all into our packed agendas. However, often the culprit is due not to a deficit of quality time but to an overabundance of wasted time. We are robbed by time bandits. Those people, places, tasks, deadlines, and obligations that steal away the time that we would rather be investing in the things we really want to do, like play golf.

Usually, when someone speaks despairingly about the amount of time it takes to play a round of golf, that person does not play. Commonly, it is someone displeased with the amount of time *someone else* is investing in the game, like a spouse, friend, or coworker. Finding enough time to play golf is about effective time management.

We *allow* ourselves to become too "busy." One of the primary areas where we lose a tremendous amount of time is in the workplace. In today's culture where it is commonplace, even celebrated, that we come in early and stay late, forego personal and vacation time, and generally devote our every waking minute to our jobs, I have a work philosophy that is, by comparison, quite radical. I believe that we have an obligation to our employers and to ourselves to give a 100 percent effort on the job. However, I do not believe that any of us should ever give 100 percent of our time to any place of employment. Most employees become proficient in a particular area, effectively becoming experts in their job functions within their places of employment. Through disciplined use of our time and effort when at work, most of us can accomplish the same amount of work, or more, in far less time. The balance of the time, the time we "pick up" by increasing our own efficiency, does not belong to the employer; it belongs to us. My opinion is that an employee's performance should be judged against productivity, not hours, and if we can assure our employers that we will hit or exceed our productivity goals, then we do not need to be shackled to a time clock. The most common day of low productivity in most workplaces is on Friday. Think about how much more time we would have to do the things we would like to do if we did not report to the office on Fridays!

The most important element to this philosophy is to identify the area where we provide a critical function and make note how much of your time is spent in that activity. It is probably less than a full workweek, and the rest of your time is spent underutilizing your capacity or kibitzing with your coworkers just because you are expected to be at the office forty or more hours a week. A recent study, compiled from employee surveys, concluded that on average, we waste more than two hours a day at work (not counting lunch or breaks).

Many employers are unable to grasp this concept of focusing on critical productivity, and not just hours worked, and if that is the case we can approach the situation by suggesting we work fewer hours (while still maintaining the same productivity levels) but accept adjusted compensation. In such a case, I recommend to my clients that they get part-time jobs in a field that interests them, thus supplementing their reduced income and benefiting from experience in an area they really enjoy.

Time bandits come in many forms, and oftentimes we ourselves are among them. While we feel like we are victims of our busyness, we fail to realize how much we are responsible for our out-of-control agendas. Take for example a small area of time that we may overlook, like vacuuming the house once a week. Make a decision to do it every other week, or every week only on weeks when the kids are out of school or you have guests. Better yet, enlist help from someone else to take this item, or similar ones, off your to-do list.

We all need to learn to say *no* a lot more often. We are not obliged to serve on every committee, board, roundtable, team, or commission that we are asked to join. This is a deceptive time bandit because when we are asked, it makes us feel good because we are needed.

Another good way to pick up extra hours is to get used to multitasking. Many of today's management books advise against multitasking, instead promoting the idea of consistently working through a to-do list to completion, one task at a time. For many, that is the most productive method. However, many things that consume our time can be done while we are working on something else. As an example, most home-based businesses require a tremendous amount of time on the telephone, either harvesting prospects or cultivating sales. With today's phone technology we could wear headsets and be free to do all kinds of other things around the house. In fact, so much technology exists today that we do not have to be tied down to an office at all, leaving us free to conduct business from wherever we are.

Perhaps the greatest time bandit of all time is procrastination. It is human nature that if we are facing a list of things to accomplish, some of which we despise doing, we will put off the unpleasant experiences for as long as possible. We can avoid them, make excuses, and justify putting these things off, but they do not go away. I employ a "worst-first" philosophy anytime I have a list of things to do. I always start with the most difficult or least enjoyable items on the list and knock them out immediately. This way, everything else I do just gets easier and more enjoyable.

We also need to remain on the lookout for our friends and coworkers who innocently rob us of time through phone calls, e-mails, and visits. Avoiding the water cooler, coffee maker, copy machine, or anywhere else people tend to stack up will save you countless precious minutes (or hours) every day. Use your caller ID, or inform your friends that during certain hours you will not

*"Perhaps the greatest time bandit
of all time is procrastination."*

answer personal e-mails or take calls because you have to devote that time to other tasks.

Finally, we should all consider a detailed one-week time tracking report. From the time we get out of bed to the minute we go back to bed at the end of the day, we should keep track of how we spend every minute. At the end of the week this exercise usually yields amazing results, showing where our time is slipping away. On average, Americans spend six hours a day watching television. Even cutting out an hour a day will pick up enough time to play almost two more rounds of golf per week!

Think about all of the ways that we could invest all of our newfound time. We could use the time to get back into shape and practice more, get a second job in a field we have always wanted to work in, like a radio station or at a golf course, or volunteer our time to coach or work with a charity. The possibilities are endless.

So the next time someone tells you that golf takes too long to play, tell them that it is nothing compared to the time they spend doing nothing.

"Putting affects the nerves more than anything. I would actually get nauseated over a three-footer."

—Byron Nelson

6

Grinding Out Self-Doubt

༕

A GAME OF INCHES

Over the course of four rounds of tournament golf, professionals traverse almost sixteen miles of terrain. It is amazing, then, that the determination of a champion can come down to a matter of inches.

Such was the case at the 1970 Open Championship at the Old Course at St. Andrews. A par save from the bunker at the difficult Road Hole meant that all Doug Sanders had to do was par the straightaway eighteenth hole, and he would win the Open and in the process hold off Jack Nicklaus, the game's most dominant golfer. The colorful Sanders, always impeccably dressed, went about navigating the seventy-second hole with a businesslike proficiency that was clearly in contrast to the artistry he employed in choosing his wardrobe. He struck a long, safe drive that left him with second-shot options including a long bump-and-run or a high soft approach. Sanders chose the latter and quite adequately left himself with a putt of some thirty feet for birdie. Putting down and across the green, Sanders' ball ended up just less than three feet from the hole, leaving him a knee-knocker putt to win the championship. The putt was downhill and breaking left to right. A putt of any length to win the Open Championship, golf's oldest major, is never an easy proposition, and Sanders' ball position and the crushing pressure surely were significant obstacles to overcome. His par putt crept toward the hole as if in slow motion. To the gasping horror of the gallery, it slid tortuously past the right lip. The result was a bogey five, and far worse, he would now face Nicklaus in a play-off the next day.

Although we could assume that Sanders spent a fitful night tossing and turning while replaying the events in his mind, certainly his performance in the play-off did not seem to be affected. Sanders was solid all day and very much a formidable opponent for Nicklaus. The match came down to the same eighteenth hole that had hosted such drama the evening before. Nicklaus was ahead by one shot. Sanders' drive had left him with the same approach position as he had had the day before. This time, ironically, he decided to play a long bump-and-run shot with a 4-iron. The ball settled some four feet from the hole. The same shot one day earlier would have likely resulted in the Open Championship. Nicklaus had struck a massive drive on the 358-yard hole that ended up past the pin in some of St. Andrews' famous and unforgiving rough. Using the combination of strength and finesse that defined his career, Nicklaus coaxed his ball to within eight feet of the cup. Nicklaus made the ensuing putt, assuring his victory, and he spontaneously tossed his putter into the air in a rare display of unbridled emotion and jubilation. The dignified Sanders congratulated the new champion and settled for his fourth second-place finish in golf's majors.

Sanders would end his playing career with twenty-one victories on the PGA Tour and Senior PGA Tour (now called Champions Tour) and second-place finishes in the 1959 PGA championship, the 1961 U.S. Open, the 1966 Open Championship, the 1970 Open Championship, and the 1987 U.S. Senior Open. Sanders would later explain his missed putt at St. Andrews by saying, "I was over the ball when I thought I saw a spot of sand on the line (of the putt). Without changing the position of my feet I bent down to pick it up, but it was a piece of brown grass. I didn't take the time to move away and get reorganized."

Time can certainly be a cruel measure, yet no other measure can be so cruel as the last thirty-six inches of a sixteen-mile trek. Golf truly is a game of mere inches.

The Three-Foot Gimme

What is it about a three-foot putt that can cause such unbridled fear?

Why is it that otherwise fearless men and women of commerce, politics, or sport become paralyzed with overwhelming anxiety when faced with such peril?

Eight-time PGA Tour winner Brad Faxon, one of the best putters on the planet, has often said that great putting is all about picking your line and confidently stroking your putt. Certainly, Brad is correct that without conviction you are leaving your effort to chance.

How then can it be that men and women who stride down the corridors of wealth and power with such confidence come to white-knuckle a shaky putter at the prospect of what any fourteen-year-old will tell you is a tap-in?

Steely nerves of youth aside, this jitters-inducing predicament is more likely the result of our own preprogramming or prequalification. *We prequalify ourselves for failure.*

The intent of this chapter is not to suggest that our misgivings are necessarily the result of an overt decision to fail, but are oftentimes the end result of a seeping assault of self-doubt. The classic three-foot putt simply provides the supreme stage upon which our all-too-common human frailty is forced from the shadows. The purpose of this chapter is to explore the roots of this gagging reflex, and to show how a better understanding can help to steady our nerves to not only perform, but excel, when our instinct may be to flee.

The chief source of our preprogramming is society itself. Think for a moment about when you were a youth and would

"Putting is like wisdom—partly a natural gift and partly the accumulation of experience."

∽ Arnold Palmer

declare your intent to do something extraordinary. More often than not your efforts would be met with doubt and ridicule. Sometimes the source of such prejudice was those closest to us, our friends and family. It is not that they deliberately wish to hold you back, but they have been programmed with the same limiting mentality as the rest of us. That is, they hold a fundamental belief that great success is something reserved for a privileged few, for those with the pedigree or rare God-given talent to rise above the great unwashed.

Consider how deeply ingrained this mentality is in our societal structure. It dates back literally centuries. In fact, it is older than golf itself. While the game of golf, or "kolf" as the ancient Dutch practitioners referred to their version more than five hundred years ago, may have a deep foundation in our Western society, it was the feudal class structure that created the division of "noble" from "common" that still lingers to this day.

Were your early efforts to rise above this structure met with words of encouragement, or a chorus of naysayers who predetermined your fate with words such as "Who does he (or she) think he is?" In other words, you do not *qualify* for greatness and achievement beyond the self-image and ingrained insecurity of the accuser. For the most part you cannot blame the accusers for they are not deliberately trying to dissuade you from your efforts. They have a greater concern that you are setting yourself up for embarrassment or discouragement at your inability to achieve heights reserved for others of greater attributes. However we justify it, we generally do not count ourselves among the privileged, and as a result of our judgment of reality, or in an effort to dissuade another from rising above that judgment, we end up in a restrictive predicament as it is predetermined that our efforts are doomed to failure.

The three-foot putt is the perfect example of how this prequalifying can play itself out in the real world. Not every missed putt is due to a deep psychological insecurity. Complete conviction and solid execution on the wrong line, regardless of your level of confidence, will not a putt make. However, more short putts,

"I don't fear death, but I sure don't like those three-footers for par."

↳ Chi Chi Rodriguez

both on and off the golf course, have been missed due to a lack of conviction than those lipped out by poor judgment.

Ben Hogan said that putting and the game of golf are actually two different games. The game of golf is played in the air, and the game of putting is played on the ground. How democratic, then, is putting! You need not be the strongest, fastest, or best-equipped, to challenge those who may be your superior in all other areas?

For most golfers, putting accounts for up to one third or more of all of the strokes they will take during a round of golf, yet golfers spend the majority of their time practicing at the range launching endless shots into the sky with fantasies that every iron shot will land so close to the hole that their competitors will simply concede the putt with a simple "pick it up." Even on the PGA Tour the reality is that the professionals make most of their birdie putts at a distance of ten or more feet, yet the spun-back iron shot that finishes inches from the hole will surely be the one to make the highlights show.

How much time are you spending working on the three-foot putts in your life? How often do you overtly or subconsciously *prequalify yourself for failure?*

"She would never go out on a date with someone like me."

"I can't apply for that job; they'd never hire me."

"I can't make this putt. I always miss them."

"I just can't beat this guy."

These self-defeating prophecies are destined to become reality because to do nothing, to choose the path of least resistance, to accept failure, is easy. In fact, you will likely be comforted by your supporters with clichés like "It's not what you know, but who you know." Well, then, get to know the right people.

Most people live their lives chained to the oars of a life of their own making whether defined by one's job, relationships, self-image, or golf game.

If we are all destined to miss our share of the three-foot putts

*"How democratic, then, is putting!
You need not be the strongest,
fastest, or best equipped, to
challenge those who may be
your superior in all other
areas."*

of life, then we can at least seek to increase our odds of success through preparation, and a conviction that not only are we capable of success but we deserve it.

Of course you will continue to have your share of rejections and failures; we all do. But over time, with consistent and persistent effort, you will find that rather than being chastised for your over-the-top efforts, you will be celebrated for them. The phrase *"Who does he think he is"* will soon be replaced with *"Who else but him?"*

"Do not be tempted to invest in a sample of each new golfing invention as soon as it makes its appearance. If you do you will only complicate and spoil your game and encumber your locker with much useless rubbish. Of course some new inventions are good, but it is usually best to wait a little while to see whether any considerable section of the golfing public approves of them before rushing to order one."

↝ Harry Vardon, 1908

7

Becoming What You Want

~

A CURRENT OF CHANGE

The history of the game of golf has been one of constant change and evolution.

From ancient herdsmen banging a rock with a stick to today's top professionals launching technologically engineered golf balls with a golf club featuring space age materials, golfers seem to be always striving to find the next great innovation to make a difficult game a little easier.

However, though change would appear to be an unstoppable current, even the earliest attempts at innovation were met with fierce resistance.

A particularly contentious episode involved two of the game's early giants, Allan Robertson and (Old) Tom Morris.

Allan Robertson is considered the game's first professional golfer. Short and powerfully compact, Robertson honed his golfing prowess over the Old Course at St. Andrews. He was widely regarded as the finest golfer of his day.

While both Robertson's grandfather and father were caddies, they also were excellent craftsmen of the feather or "featherie" golf balls. The skill was passed on to Allan Robertson as well, and he became highly proficient in the production of featherie golf balls.

"Never have a club in your bag that you are afraid to hit."

᠕ Tom Kite

The process of producing a featherie was neither easy nor quick. It involved stuffing boiled goose feathers into a tiny leather pouch, then sewing the seam shut. The wet leather would shrink as the feathers dried and expanded. This conflicting action would produce a small, hard ball that could be driven a relatively long way. The shortcomings of the featherie ball were that over repeated uses the hand-sewn seams would break open and lose shape, and that they were very expensive due to the time it took to produce them.

One of the most dramatic technological shifts in the game's history took place in the late 1840s when a St. Andrews doctor received a piece of art from the Far East. It was wrapped in a protective coat of gutta-percha, which had a texture roughly like our modern-day rubber. Gutta-percha is a byproduct of a tropical tree. It was soon discovered that the substance could be heated and shaped like a golf ball. The benefits were obvious, including durability, much lower cost, and, after some tweaking, superior workability and overall performance.

As one might imagine, Allan Robertson despised the new ball that challenged his featherie ball business. He required all of his employees to declare an oath to the featherie ball, hoping that their collective disdain and his own powerful reputation would discredit the "gutty" ball.

One of Robertson's workers was Tom Morris, later to be known as "Old Tom." The two were a formidable partnership in business and in particular on the golf course. Both possessed the ability to persevere through crushing pressure and the golfing skills to match. As things developed, the two skilled, strong-willed indi-viduals would ultimately find themselves on opposite sides of the current of change defined by the upstart gutty ball.

Tom Morris was reportedly intrigued by the gutty ball and tried it in a practice round. When Robertson found out about Morris' breach of confidence, he sacked him.

Morris, in turn, set up his own shop just off the eighteenth green at the Old Course (the shop still exists today) and quickly established a vibrant business. As to the gutty ball, it would become the dominant golf ball technology for almost the next fifty years. The driving forces of change are not new to the game, and, regardless of the forces or agendas arrayed against it, change will happen.

As for Robertson, he eventually warmed up to the new ball, even reportedly improving its performance by discovering that by hammering a primitive dimple pattern into the ball's surface it would help the ball's flight trajectory and control, particularly in windy conditions. He also made amends with Morris, and the two continued to defeat all teams that were brazen (or foolish) enough to challenge the duo that never lost a match.

Transformation

The process of creating a set of irons fascinates me. To think that a piece of metal can be transformed into a beautiful and highly useful tool leaves an equipment geek such as me to marvel at the work of art that has been created.

The process starts in the fertile mind of a club designer and progresses to a drafting table or a CAD system. Soon the image of what the designer wants the iron to look like starts to become clear. The vast majority of iron heads today feature a perimeter-weighted cavity intended to maximize forgiveness on off-center hits. This concept became the accepted form of iron design in a category called "game improvement" irons over thirty years ago, with the release of the first Ping irons. Cavity-back irons represent more than 95 percent of all irons purchased each year.

Prior to cavity-back irons, the irons of choice for over one hundred years were forged. The forging of an iron is an amazing process to watch. For hundreds of years, the process was the same as making a sword; the iron head was literally hammered into form through fire, grit, artistry, and brute strength. Taking a stroll through a display of antique clubs makes you realize that everything new is old again, because there are virtually no new technological designs that have not been tried over the years. Perimeter weighting, bore-through shafts, low centers of gravity, oversized heads, face inserts—they have all been attempted thousands of times as club designers have tried to find that perfect club that will turn a weak slice into a commanding draw. The differences today are the design and manufacturing equipment available to manipulate metal and the new space-age materials that clubmakers can now employ. Forged irons are still being produced, generally for low-handicap golfers and professionals,

"We must embrace change to grow, learn and advance, or we die."

but they are now pressed into form by massive machines that employ thousands of pounds of pressure per square inch with each compression. For my money, there is no more beautiful golf club than a chromed, carbon steel forged iron head.

For the cavity-back iron, the next step after the drafting table is to produce an exact wax model of the club. Everything, right down to the letters and numbers in the cavity and the grooves on the face, is precisely carved into the wax. Next, the wax model has liquid ceramic poured over it until the ceramic dries, entombing the wax within it. The ceramic is then heated, the melted wax is poured out, and what is left is an exact ceramic mold or cavity of the iron head. Pour in the molten stainless steel, let it cool and harden, then break away the ceramic coat and you have your iron. This process is called precision casting, and it is quite an amazing and exacting process. In its way, the transformation is as unexpected as that of a spring butterfly emerging from the cocoon.

Embracing the need for transformation in our lives can be a daunting predicament. Almost all of us have some area of our lives that should, or must, change. Perhaps you have come to the conclusion that a relationship needs to change if it is to continue, or you have lost your interest in your current job and want to change careers. No doubt, making a change is hard and scary. Change not only incites our insecurities, it also encompasses an altered self-image that causes tension and stress. It is for these reasons that many people choose to ignore the need to change. The sad reality is that most people will continue to live out their days unfulfilled in a life of *their* choosing.

The world is changing all the time, and it will happen whether we wish to be a part of it or not. We must embrace change to grow, learn, and advance, or we die.

I believe that change comes in these stages:

Honesty: Being truthful about what changes we need to make in our lives. Usually, we all know what we need to do, we just need to summon up the courage to do it.

"The drive is to always get better. No matter what, you never get there. It's a never-ending struggle. That's the fun of it, no matter how good you play, you can always play better, which makes it exciting the next day."

∽ Tiger Woods

The Total Commitment Contract: Make a 100 percent commitment to change. It is a promise to yourself. Write it down, date it, and sign it. Have a completion date, as with any other contract. It will help train your mind and bolster your resolve to keep the commitment. Review it at the start of every day.

Have a Plan: Know what you want to accomplish with your change and when you want to accomplish it.

Get Help: The paths we walk in life are well worn before us. Reach out to others who have gone through similar experiences. Support groups, counseling, libraries, and the Internet can be valuable tools to ease our journey.

Stand Guard: We all know our weaknesses, so be on the outlook for procrastination, denial, and excuses.

Take Action: EVERY DAY and NO MATTER WHAT. Taking action does not have to involve major steps, but even small efforts every day will eventually help us reach our goals.

With commitment, hard work, and persistence we can accomplish amazing transformations in our lives. Transformations as hard as steel.

"You're never too old to play golf. If you can walk, you can play."

ৎৄ Louise Suggs

8

Footsteps of Champions

⤳

CHASING GIANTS

Often, our heroes are so much larger than life that we expect them to be nothing less than giants. By any measure, Ben Hogan and Byron Nelson were giants of the game. Therefore, it is impressive that in 1956 a couple of young amateurs would challenge them to a match when the professionals, both in their mid-forties, still possessed the skills that numbered them among the game's all-time elite. Between them, Hogan and Nelson had won fourteen major championships by this time.

Ken Venturi and Harvie Ward were the two brash young amateurs who apparently believed that the best way to follow in the footsteps of giants is to walk alongside them in head-to-head competition.

Venturi, who was twenty-five, had only recently returned from a tour of duty in Korea, where he was an infantry sergeant. While Venturi may have been destined for golfing greatness (two years later, in 1958, he led the Masters as an amateur after three rounds; he won the 1964 U.S. Open in dramatic fashion; and he had a long and distinguished career as the lead golf analyst for CBS Sports), in 1956 he held the reputation as being one of the finest amateur golfers in the United States. Obviously, Venturi knew well the status of the two men they were about to compete against, but his relationship with them was more than just pass-

"The guy who believes in happy endings is going to play consistently better golf than the man who approaches every act of existence with fear and foreboding."

ॐ Tony Lema

ing knowledge. Venturi modeled his game after Byron Nelson, and he considered Nelson his mentor. Venturi also revered Hogan, and it appeared even this early in Venturi's career that Hogan had great affection for him as well. Two years earlier, Hogan had reportedly set up Venturi with a set of Hogan clubs.

Harvie Ward, who was thirty-one, was the reigning U.S. Amateur champion (he would win the crown again later that year), the 1949 NCAA champion, the 1952 British Amateur champion, and the 1954 Canadian Amateur champion, and he had played on the 1953 and 1955 Walker Cup teams (he would play again in 1959).

So Hogan and Nelson not only knew of their competition, but also realized that these two amateurs had the ability to give them a good fight. In fact, it is probably a sign of the respect the two professionals had for Venturi and Ward that they would even agree to the match, because they really had nothing to gain and everything to lose. If they won, it was expected, and if they lost, it would be an embarrassment to lose to amateurs.

Just exactly how the match came to pass and a number of other facts about the event are shrouded in the kind of Hoganesque mystery that seems to surround so many events in his life. The most common explanation for how the match came to be was that Eddie Lowery, who caddied for Francis Ouimet in the 1913 U.S. Open at Brookline and who owned a San Francisco–area car dealership where Venturi and Ward worked, set up the match with help from George Coleman, a wealthy Texas businessman who was close to Hogan and Nelson. It was agreed that the match would be solely for pride, and no money was knowingly wagered or exchanged. The match would be played at Cypress Point Golf Club.

The exact date of the match is also not completely clear, but it is assumed that it was played a few days before Bing Crosby's Pro-Am at Pebble Beach. In fact, Hogan is said to have made a decoy tee time for a practice round at Pebble Beach the morning of the match in order to keep fans and media off their track.

"Sure, I believe in ghosts. I know there are ghosts at St. Andrews. When you walk across the Swilcan Bridge you can almost see them, they're so close. The Morrises, the Auchterlonies, I'm certain they're all flying around out there."

— Lee Trevino

What is indisputable is that the two amateurs came out on fire. Venturi and Ward had birdies on nine of the first ten holes. However, despite this impressive start, they still found themselves one down to Hogan and Nelson thanks to an 85-yard pitch-in for eagle by Hogan on the uphill, 500-yard, par-5 tenth hole. On the 450-yard, par-4 eleventh hole, Nelson used a 2-iron to set up a 12-foot birdie putt, only to be matched by his protégé Venturi.

The match continued in this fashion in what may have been the finest display of golf ever seen in match-play competition. *Golf Magazine* once referred to this match as "the greatest golf match ever played."

Hogan and Venturi matched birdies on the par-3, fifteenth. When the players reached the famous 235-yard, par-3, sixteenth hole, the professionals were still clinging to their one-shot lead. On this day, the sixteenth, which sits like Atlantis amidst the rocks and crashing waves, was playing dead into a harsh Pacific wind. Nelson and Ward were both forced to use drivers to reach the putting surface. In a testament to their prowess, their tee shots set up birdie putts that both men would convert.

The seventeenth hole was halved, setting up the short, 342-yard, par-4, eighteenth hole as the deciding factor. Venturi and Ward's only chance was for another birdie, hoping that the professionals would score a par, at best. Venturi negotiated his wedge approach shot to within 12 feet of the cup. In a microcosm of the day, Hogan hit his approach just inside of Venturi's. Venturi then displayed nerves of steel when he smoothly rolled his ball into the hole. Hogan surveyed his putt with the intensity that earned him the nickname of "The Hawk." As he settled over the putt, it is reported that Hogan growled through clenched teeth, "I'm not about to be tied by two goddamn amateurs." Even the golf ball would not risk enduring Hogan's wrath as it split the center of the hole and dropped for a birdie, ensuring the professionals' victory.

In keeping with the Hogan legend, the match was reported to have taken place in near total silence except for the occasional

"You're away." In addition, no known scorecard from this match exists. Byron Nelson later noted he did not know whether any of the players kept a scorecard, and that a scorecard was unnecessary anyway, because both sides knew exactly where they stood throughout the match.

Ward and Nelson ended up shooting scores of 67. Venturi shot a 65 and Hogan a 63. The amateurs better-ball score was 59, the professionals', a 58. As a foursome, they had twenty-seven birdies and one eagle.

~~~

Following in the Footsteps
of Champions

Golf is a game that embraces mysticism and the general existence of ghosts as commonplace.

However, these otherworldly manifestations can take various forms. Some sense the awesome weight of history that has occurred at a particular golf course they may be playing. To stride down the same fairway as the game's legends, perhaps to relive the scene of some famous shot or trace the undulations of a green where Jones, Hogan, Snead, or even Palmer, Nicklaus, Watson, or Woods accomplished some seemingly superhuman feat. You see, in golf, the ghost of a legend need not take the form of someone who has died. No, the specters of their great accomplishments almost seem to take on an immortal existence separate from the mortal man. Take Nicklaus hitting the pin on the seventeenth hole at Pebble Beach in the 1972 U.S. Open, or Watson's chip-in from the rough on the same hole, against Nicklaus, in the 1982 U.S. Open as examples.

To others, the game provides a time portal where one is transported back to the ghosts of joys and frustrations of a distant golfing past as if in some Dickens' Christmas classic. Think about the last time you played a golf course that you had not played in years. Surely the currents of life have rushed you far from the point where you began your long walk with the game? Was yours perhaps a hometown municipal or "muni" course? Maybe it was your father's country club, where he took you out golfing at a "real club" for the first time, or perhaps where you beat your dad for the first time (when you think back on it now, are you sure he did not *let* you win)? What's more, perhaps your golfing psyche still

"What is this old, abandoned golf course?"

~ Sam Snead, when he
saw St. Andrews for
the first time

bears the scar of some long ago injury. Perhaps you have returned to a course that was the scene of the loss of an important match, or an embarrassing score or shot?

The game is often called a "game of a lifetime" as a precursor to stating that one can play and enjoy the game for the rest of your life. But in golf, "a lifetime" can mean far more than simply peering ahead. The game of golf is as much about the past as it is about the present and the future. In fact, the three become so intertwined that it is often hard to distinguish one from the next. In the following chapter we will explore the ease with which we not only accept, but also embrace, the ghosts of the game of golf, yet we do not always recognize the ghosts we walk with in our daily lives. These unseen apparitions may be ghosts of neglect, regret, failure, or uncertainty. Learning to identify these personal ghosts is an important step in helping you to vanquish them from holding you back from reaching your goals.

Fittingly, there is no other course in the world that seems to embody a mystical realm more so than the "Home of Golf," the Old Course at St. Andrews. In Michael Murphy's definitive book about golf's mystical and transcendental properties, *Golf in the Kingdom*, he notes that it has been said that the eighteenth hole at the fictional "Burningbush," just like St. Andrews, is built upon an ancient graveyard. How appropriate, then, that for every account we know of some great triumph upon that spot, so too does the dream of another die?

St. Andrews the city and the Old Course in particular are so much more than merely a golfing destination. For a golfer, St. Andrews is quite simply a mecca. It is a pilgrimage that anyone who truly purports to love the game must make at least once in a lifetime.

Aside from a battlefield or other locale of intense human drama, there is perhaps no more haunted a place in the world than St. Andrews. The aura of what has gone before you embraces you as soon as you enter the ancient city. From the massive cathedral ruins to the rubble of the St. Andrews castle, each element of the city seems to be a building block of anticipation to your

"I could take out of my life everything except my experiences at St. Andrews and I'd still have a rich, full life."

⤳ Bobby Jones

first steps on to the historic course. It is almost overwhelming, and well worth it for a first-time pilgrim to walk the course the evening before a round, if only to confirm that your feet really do touch the earth.

No one walks alone down these storied links. It starts with the Old Course's famous Scottish urban setting, defined by the noble if stoic R & A building and the surrounding city streets. It includes the watchful presence of Old Tom Morris' still-in-operation golf shop, just a wedge shot from the eighteenth green. It continues with one's every step down the hardened fairways, embraced by echoes of the legions of galleries from championships past as you literally walk in the footsteps of the game's heroes, knowing that the turf you tread is the same that every great golfer the game has ever known (except Hogan) has humbly strode along.

Of course you want to shoot a good score at the Old Course, but interestingly, at the end of the day, your score is of little consequence. As you cross the uneven rocks of the Swilken Bridge and eventually putt out to the scattered, yet polite applause of the ever-present gallery of the reverent, you realize one of the great truths of the game. The game of golf does not define *how* you must enjoy it. In fact, the most enjoyable rounds of golf come when we shed the conventional, defined measures of golf and elevate a game of numbers to an experience of contentment and joy. Think about your most enjoyable golfing experiences—did they happen the day you simply shot a great score, or was it an occasion on a higher plane when the magic of a special place converged with the warmth of companionship and the spirit of contentment?

It comes as no surprise that often these same rounds of golf usually end up being days of solid performance against par, or an opponent, because you were unencumbered by haunting anxiety.

Why is it that we promote golf's great connection to the ghosts of its past and allow ourselves to use these powerful images to

"No one will ever have golf under his thumb. No round ever will be so good it could not have been better. Perhaps this is why golf is the greatest of games."

↬ Bobby Jones

enlighten us on the links, yet we often fail to channel the same positive energy from the ghostly realms of our own world?

What ghosts of your past are haunting your performance? Why do we allow them such latitude? And who are the legends that lurk in your own past, waiting to offer you contentment and calm?

The game of golf teaches us that whether the fairway in your life is covered with grass or marble, all of the legends of any field of endeavor strode down the same pathways as you and faced the same hazards. Did strong winds and heavy rains of rejection and insecurity threaten to blow their goals out of bounds? Yet they succeeded. Through a combination of commitment, purpose, and perseverance, they were able to vanquish their own ghosts of doubt and use the examples of their heroes to carry them onward.

Seek out those who have distinguished themselves in your chosen field. Find out how they did it, and what they did to overcome adversity along the way. Embrace their accomplishments with the same awe as you would the feats of your favorite golfing legends.

One of the most effective and easiest ways to learn from the champions that predated you is to read every biography you can. Biographies are like recipes of how to succeed. Interestingly, you may find that their pathways to success usually follow similar paths of vision, commitment, perseverance, and hard work.

It may be time to replace your old ghosts with new ones. To realize that your heroes, the legends of your particular world, did not simply attain an unreachable mark, but in fact have forged a path before you.

Do not be afraid, follow the path; you will not be walking alone.

"If it were not for you, Walter, this dinner tonight would be downstairs in the pro shop and not in the ballroom."

ꝩ Arnold Palmer to Walter Hagen

9

The Pay-for-Play Game

ॐ

GUT CHECK

The dawn of the 1914 U.S. Open saw the national championship bathed in an entirely new light. Francis Ouimet's unlikely victory at The Country Club one year before had propelled the Championship, and the game, to new heights of popularity.

One would assume that such a prominent stage would be the perfect showcase for a extroverted young professional from the Country Club of Rochester named Walter Hagen.

Hagen had done a great deal of soul-searching in the year since Ouimet's victory had thrust the young amateur to the rare level of greatness. It was not Ouimet's success that had discouraged Hagen. What had frustrated him was the fact that he missed out on the play-off by the slim margin of one stroke. Instead of taking solace in the fact that he had been that close, instead he viewed that single stroke as an obstacle as big as a mountain and as an omen that he might need to look elsewhere to find his greatness.

Disillusioned by his golfing prospects, Hagen actually spent the winter prior to the 1914 U.S. Open in Florida, where he went through spring training with the Philadelphia Nationals. A fine all-around athlete, Hagen performed adequately and fully expected that his future would include pitching in semi-professional baseball to augment his position as a golf professional.

"Golf is good for the soul. You get so mad at yourself you forget to hate your enemies."

⌇ Will Rogers

However, upon returning to Rochester, Hagen was greeted with a membership whose enthusiasm for his prior year's near miss and pride that Hagen was "their pro" meant that not entering the 1914 U.S. Open was not an option. This was despite Hagen's enlightened vision of golf's newfound place in his life. In fact, so enthused were the membership that member Earnest Willard the editor of the local *Democrat and Chronicle* newspaper, agreed to pay for Hagen's expenses.

The trip from Rochester to Chicago was not particularly arduous, even by 1914 standards, and Hagen arrived in time to prepare for the Open with some practice rounds at Midlothian.

On the eve of the first day of the tournament, Hagen did something that, while it seemed perfectly natural to him, would underscore the persona of one of the game's great champions and characters. That night, Hagen satisfied his highbrow tastes by proudly venturing out for a lobster dinner. While it was not out of character, the young golfer's decision involved two problems. First, shipping seafood around the country in 1914 was no easy task, and lobsters do not come from Lake Michigan. And second, the high life Hagen was aspiring to live with this meal was on a low-dollar budget. That combination would prove fateful as the less-than-fresh crustacean would get the final revenge.

That night, before retiring, Hagen would feel the first pains of what any one of us would identify with a shrug as "maybe something I ate." But, by the wee hours of the morning, Hagen was in the throes of a full-blown intestinal tempest. By first light Hagen could hardly stand.

Once more, the prospect of not competing in the 1914 U.S. Open seemed to be the only logical choice, and once more the weight of expectation and obligation to his membership constituency would force him to carry on to Midlothian.

Surely Hagen must have questioned his decision, and his sanity, when he boarded the South Shore train to take him to Midlothian. As well-chronicled as the severe winds and arctic chills of a Chicago winter may be, summers in the Windy City can be as sweltering as the African plains. So it was on this day as the heat and humidity were coupled with black soot, belching from the stream engine and hanging like a coat in the open car's lifeless air.

The ashen and visibly ailing Hagen would shuffle to the first tee free of the weight of expectation. Rather, his weary mind was forced to concentrate on how horrible he felt. His round would start out up and down, much as he had spent the night before. However, swashbuckling champion that he was, the talented Hagen would consistently follow up each wayward shot with a miraculous one. By the end of the morning eighteen, Hagen would post a course record 68 and lead the 1914 U.S. Open by one shot over defending champion Francis Ouimet.

Hagen's spirit was lifted by his ability to persevere despite his ailment, and in the afternoon round, when course conditions were more difficult, Hagen hung on for a score of 74 and a share of the lead with Tom McNamara, three shots clear of Ouimet.

Hagen played it down the middle with steak and potatoes that night for dinner, satisfied with the outcome of a difficult day.

The next day Hagen awoke feeling physically restored, and he posted morning and afternoon rounds of 75 and 73, respectively, tying the Open mark set by George Sargent five years earlier.

McNamara and Ouimet both faded over the final thirty-six holes. Hagen's only real challenge came from the amateur sensation Chick Evans, who despite his inspired play finished one shot shy of catching Hagen.

The 1914 U.S. Open victory opened up a world of potential for the engaging Hagen as offers for golfing exhibitions came pouring in. One of the smartest men ever to play the game, and an opportunistic showman, Hagen was one of the all-time great golfing entertainers. He was also one of the first professional golfers to grasp the reality that people were willing to pay for the privilege of being in the company of someone who had the ability to work magic with a golf ball.

Obviously, being a part-time baseball player would not have

Fairways of Life

afford him the standard of living and fame that he was destined to achieve in golf. In addition, all professional golfers owe a debt of gratitude to Hagen, for he was the man that opened the door of status to the generations of golfers who followed. His personality demanded that he be at the center of the clubhouse cocktail party rather than simply toiling in the golf shop or changing his shoes in his car.

Hagen would go on to win another ten major championships in his career, with the 1914 U.S. Open doubtless paving the way.

Hagen's victory proves that the first step to being a champion is simply showing up.

"Golf has probably kept more people sane than psychiatrists have."

➹ Harvey Penick

꒰ꜛ

The Pay-for-Play Game

One of the things that make golf unique is that professional golfers are independent contractors. Play well, you get paid. Miss the cut, and you get nothing. I cannot think of a situation that is more reflective of a free market than that.

The same cannot be said for team professional sports. In fact, most of us have become numb to the mind-blowing contracts that players are signing today. Granted, sports are entertainment and if you can get it, well, I can't see a player's agent turning the money away. However, you would be hard-pressed to find anyone who would not agree (including most of the players) that paying a professional athlete a *guaranteed* salary of hundreds of thousands of dollars *per week* while we continue to lay off teachers due to tight school budgets is a poor reflection of where our priorities lie as a society.

In addition, most of these contracts are based upon a *promise* to perform. If a player becomes hurt or fails to play to his or her ability level, the money is not adjusted, although it may affect their negotiating power the next time.

Such is not the case with golfers. While professional golfers are well paid for what they earn on tour, the critical reality is that *they have to earn it*, just like you and me, and in that regard we are all independent contractors.

When you think about it, most of our frustrations with our places of employment come from not being recognized for the depth of the contributions we make to the company, through being forced to "clean up the mess" made by somebody else, enduring undefined and frequently changing directives, endless meetings, inequity, and favoritism, and not being paid what

"Don't play too much golf. Two rounds a day are plenty."

♪ Harry Vardon

we are worth. It is particularly easy to get caught up in the group commiseration and low morale that these situations (and dozens of others) cause in the workplace.

However, it does not have to be that way. Most workplace discontent and low morale come from our own expectation of how things *should* be. Are most work places poorly managed and lacking in clear strategic objectives? Yes. Does most of the stress and tension caused by this reality get placed squarely on the shoulders of the employees? Yes, again, but only if *you* let it.

I prefer to embrace an "independent contractor's mentality" toward whomever I am working for. Look at it this way: if you were an attorney, and you had a client that was paying you $100,000 per year, you would take that client's phone call if he called you at 3:00 A.M. Sunday morning, wouldn't you? What's more, your personal like or dislike of the client would not matter, nor would you care whether they gave you a pat on the back every now and then, because the best affirmation of your good performance is the receipt of the client's check.

It does not matter whom we work for or what we do. The reality is that we are all independent contractors. Each of us, individually, is like a mini corporation, the *Me Corporation*. As *Me Corporation* we have money coming in from what we earn (revenue), and we have bills to pay (expenses), and at the end of the year we hope to have put something away into our savings (profit).

Therefore, it is important to remember that we owe it to ourselves, our spouses, and our loved ones—our "stockholders"—to continue to perform to our potential. We need to work diligently to establish the quality, value, and accountability of the product or service we provide. It is critical that we avoid constant complaining because the belief that we have a *right* to complain comes from a sense of entitlement about the power we have as employees. This is a dangerous trap, for the modern workplace has proven again and again that entitlement does not secure employment, only performance does. If you view your product or service in the manner of an independent contractor, as the *Me*

Corporation, then you will take pride in what you produce and recognize that the coworkers whom you are measured against (your competition in this regard) are denigrating the value of their product by tearing down their employer (your client) and illogically hoping that a poor effort and attitude will somehow cause their bosses to start appreciating them.

There are some action steps that we can take to help establish our *Me Corporation*. First of all, establish a mission statement.

Having a personal *mission statement* helps to keep us focused and to realize that what we do for work need not only be a means to an end (making money), but can also be enriching and important. We should strive to make our mission statements as focused on our core values as possible, but even a very broad statement such as, "To make the world a better place" gives us direction.

Next, construct a *business plan*. Most people do not create a plan of what they hope to accomplish in the coming year. Rather, they allow a manager or supervisor to define how performance is to be measured. No one knows our potential better than we do. We should craft our own definitions of success. We may even consider sharing our views with our bosses. If you feel that you are constantly "over managed" by your supervisor, then after this exercise he or she will find it much harder to push your buttons of insecurity. The hardest people to manage through domination are those who hold themselves to a standard of excellence beyond that which anyone else would even consider.

Finally, consider *diversifying and investing in the Me Corporation*. Consider getting other part-time work in a field we have always wanted to be a part of, or volunteer with a worthy charity. Our investment could take the form of going back to school, or taking courses for greater proficiency, or even learning a new trade. It also takes the form of joining professional organizations. Networking in this regard is an invaluable asset.

Yes, the idea of being an independent contractor is scary because the safety net is gone. But the reality is that in our modern workplace there are no safety nets.

You may be apprehensive about the concept of being an independent contractor, but you already are one. The question is, will you be a champion and perform to your greatest potential, or do you run the risk of missing the cut?

The Back Nine

"I was lucky to win. I've never been happier to get any cup, and I never worked so hard nor suffered so much, either."

∼ Bobby Jones, on his
1930 British Amateur
victory

10

Making Your Own Luck

LADY FORTUNE

Sometimes the pathway to success is lined with deep rough, unforgiving hazards, and heartless competition. It takes a firm view of the end goal, steely nerves, and occasionally good, old-fashioned luck to hoist the champion's trophy.

Luck can be an ambiguous asset, for it has two sides. Some choose to dwell on the negative consequences of its seemingly random application, while golfers like the great Bobby Jones learned to harness its opportunities.

Such was the case with Jones' improbable march to the "Impregnable Quadrilateral," the Grand Slam in 1930. Without Jones' ability to remain patient until luck, or, as he called it, "Lady Fortune," turned his way, he would not be remembered today as the author of one of the greatest feats in the history of the game.

Due to the fact that Jones' conquest took place over seventy-five years ago, it is easy to discount its significance. It is only natural that we should rationalize and discount his accomplishment by measuring it against those of the time we live in. Many today mistakenly believe that because two of Jones' majors that year were amateur competitions (the British Amateur and U.S. Amateur), he did not face truly world-class competition. However, this judgment is blinded by the bias of our own age. During

Jones' era, professional golf was not what it is today. Professional golfers were not the media mega-stars and multimillionaires that they are today. Being a professional in the first half of the twentieth century (at least before Hagen and others completely altered the image of a touring professional golfer) was akin to a service position. A pro attended to support tasks such as club repair and lessons, playing an occasional round of golf when duties at the country club did not prohibit it. Therefore, it was not uncommon that many of the world's finest golfers chose to remain amateurs—such as Jones and Chick Evans, for example. It is true that Jones' amateur status meant that he maintained his game in world-class form while playing about as often as today's average weekend golf enthusiast, due to the demands of first his education, and later his law practice.

It is also unfair to assume that due to shorter, less-manicured golf courses and the idiosyncrasies of the equipment of Jones' era, including hickory shafts (steel shafts had been introduced to the game by this time, but Jones, who could drive the ball an impressive 250 yards, chose to continue using his trusted hickory shafts for his run to the Grand Slam), a score of par or better in 1930 does not represent the same accomplishment as it does in our day. To the contrary, the inherent deficiencies, irregularities, and inconsistencies of the equipment and course conditions during his time would suggest that his scores are even more impressive than meets the eye. Can you imagine what a player of Jones' caliber would do with our modern golf equipment!

Finally, over the decades, the image of Bobby Jones has grown to such a dimension that many believe that he rolled to each of his championships with little or no formidable competition. This too is fallacy. Jones was the greatest golfer in the world at his peak; there can be little doubt about that. However, his capturing of the Grand Slam was as much a story of vision, determination, and overcoming adversity as it was of dominance. His success can be viewed as the unstoppable progress of inevitable fate, for his golf skills were that consummate—yet he simply would not have won the Grand Slam without some very fortuitous breaks.

Innately, he possessed the will and fortitude to use these developments to his gain.

Great examples of how he seized on opportunities exist in events that took place in the Open Championship at Royal Liverpool (Hoylake) and at the U.S. Open at Interlachen.

Two weeks prior to the Open Championship, Jones had secured the first leg of the Grand Slam by winning the British Amateur at St. Andrews. As great courses tend to produce great champions, Jones' march to victory in the match-play event was not without its trials. It can be argued that Jones won the British Amateur as much with his intellect as with his immense golfing talent. This point was particularly illustrated in his fourth-round match against defending champion Cyril Tolley, who was Jones' opposite in almost every manner. The massive Tolley was capable of overpowering a golf course and intimidating his opponents. Jones craftily used a psychological strategy that turned Tolley's strengths into weaknesses (Jones really had Tolley's number. See Jones vs. Tolley in the 1926 Walker Cup on p. 9.) and posted a hard fought victory by winning the eighteenth hole (with a stymie). However, while Jones left St. Andrews with the coveted victory, he also left with the knowledge that he had not played to his fullest potential. If he was to continue his march to the Grand Slam, he would need to be ready for the Open.

The pressure that was starting to mount on Bobby Jones at this point was formidable. Perhaps in an effort to help clear his head, after the British Amateur victory, Jones took a holiday in Paris with his wife Mary for a few days of relaxation. When he arrived at Hoylake for the Open, his game did not immediately follow. Jones held it together well enough, however, to qualify adequately and hoped that he would find his touch in the championship.

Jones bogeyed two of his first three holes to start the Open. As with Tiger Woods at Major championships, some of Jones' troubles can be accounted to the fact that a photographer insisted on taking his picture while he was in his setup or backswing. Eventually, Jones steadied himself and posted a 2-under-par

"When you work very hard, you get lucky. And when they say you're lucky, that's when you know you have arrived."

♫ Chi Chi Rodriguez

70, sharing the lead with Mac Smith and Henry Cotton. Jones would post a 72 in the second round and lead the tournament by one over Fred Robson.

At this time, the final two rounds of the Open were contested as thirty-six holes on the last day. Jones' third round would begin as his first round did, with two bogies over the first three holes. Jones, would end up posting a score of 74, 2 over par. Archie Compston, a 6-foot-5 Welshman, was playing a few holes behind Jones, and he was tearing it up. Compston would post bookend scores of 34 going out and coming in, and would end the round with the course record and a one-shot lead on Jones as they prepared for the final eighteen holes.

It was during this final round that Jones seemed to have come back into the good graces of "Lady Fortune." Jones' tee shot on the second hole was badly sliced, and the ball sailed directly for the out of bounds. But before it met its doom, the ball connected soundly with the head of a marshal and rebounded wildly into a bunker on the adjacent fourteenth hole. Jones knew that fate had granted him a mulligan, and he capitalized on the opportunity by making birdie.

Jones would par the third hole to stand at even par for the round and the tournament as his closest pursuer, Compston, who had teed off almost an hour behind Jones, was sizing up a tap-in putt on the first hole for par. Compston was brimming with confidence, still riding the hot streak from his morning round. The less-than-two-foot putt that awaited Compston was nothing more than routine, and the large man carelessly stabbed at the putt to clean up his par. To his horror, his unconcerned effort left the ball perched on the edge of the cup, and he was forced to settle for a bogey. The incident seemed to unnerve Compston, and his game quickly fell apart; he eventually posted a score of 82.

The implosion of Compston did not translate into an automatic victory for Jones, for the great man did little to help his cause. On the short par-5 eighth hole, which Jones had birdied in each previous round, he not only failed to get up and down for birdie from just off the green, but he chunked two chip shots,

"If I happen to start out with four fives, I simply figure that I've used up my quota. I forget them and start out on a new track."

ᕲ Walter Hagen

missed a par-saving putt, and then missed the bogey putt to post a 7, the highest score he ever shot in an Open championship.

Jones' troubles were not over yet, as he posted bogey on the eleventh, thirteenth, and fifteenth holes. But on the par-5 sixteenth hole, Jones seemed to call upon the magic that defined his career. Jones hit his second shot into a bunker at the left front of the green, and his ball settled into a difficult position on a downhill lie. Jones was forced into an awkward stance with one leg in the bunker and one out. But he executed a perfect shot, exploding the ball softly up over the bunker face and rolling it directly toward the hole for a two-inch tap-in birdie.

Jones' final-round 75 and total of 3 over par was good enough to win the Open Championship with a two-shot victory over Leo Diegel and Mac Smith, a victory that would not have happened without some good old-fashioned luck.

Back in the United States to continue his march toward the Grand Slam, Jones' game seemed to be coming back around to a standard he expected. Perhaps being back on familiar American soil had something to do with it, but it was more likely the result of having more time to practice.

After the first round of the U.S. Open at Interlachen Country Club in suburban Minneapolis, Jones found himself one shot off the lead after posting a solid 1-under-par score of 71.

Jones began the second round in a similar fashion, needing only a par on the par-5 ninth hole to go out in 1 under par. The hole measured less than 500 yards, and it was possible to get home in two if the second shot was played over a pretty lake distinguished by beautiful lilies. Jones approached the hole with an air of confidence, as he had consistently birdied it in his practice rounds. Jones' drive was slightly pushed, and his ball settled into a barren spot near the front of the lake. Jones, still determined to get his second shot on the green, took aim over the large body of water. At the top of his backswing, Jones' peripheral vision picked up two young girls darting out of the gallery ahead of him. In a fraction of a second, his mind raced to react, and the resultant

"I'm a lucky dog. You got to be lucky to beat Jack Nicklaus, because he's the greatest golfer who ever held a club."

∽ Lee Trevino, after
defeating Nicklaus
in a play-off at the
1971 U.S. Open

swing nearly topped the ball, sending it on a knee-high trajectory that was clearly destined to land in the lake.

Once more, good fortune seemed to be smiling on Bobby Jones. His ball skipped twice over the lake and bounded its way up to a grassy area some ninety feet short of the green. Many swore that Jones' ball was the beneficiary of a fortuitous bounce off of one of the lily pads, although Jones consistently denied such assistance. What could not be denied was that a shot that clearly should have led to a bogey, or worse, now lay near the green in two. Jones would once more take advantage of the opportunity by posting a birdie on the hole, and he ended up finishing the round at 1 over par.

Jones posted a dominating score of 68 in the third round and hung on for a tumultuous 75 in the final round. His score was good enough for a two-stroke victory over Mac Smith, securing the third leg of the Grand Slam.

Of course, Jones would complete his quest for the Grand Slam with his victory in the U.S. Amateur at Merion. Jones' conquest in the match-play event, seemed to be predetermined, and he coasted to a convincing victory. Having accomplished golf's ultimate feat and weary of the expectations that he would win every time he teed it up, Jones would retire at the age of twenty-eight.

Bobby Jones deserves every accolade bestowed upon him, but it is likely that even he would have admitted that no matter how good you are, it helps not only to be lucky, but to know how to take advantage of it.

"I didn't win in the 1930s because I hadn't yet learned to concentrate, to ignore the gallery and the other golfers, and to shut my mind against everything but my own game."

᠕ Ben Hogan

∂

With My Luck . . .

One would think that an Irishman named Murphy must have been a golfer, for his wisdom forms the bedrock of many a golfer's psychology. Murphy's Law—"If anything can go wrong, it will"— illustrates a common victim mentality that permeates nearly all levels of competitive golf. It can be safely assumed that in every round of golf ever played, one or more golfers in the foursome, while watching their balls in flight, were heard to mutter dejectedly, "With my luck . . . the ball will land in a divot . . . bounce out of bounds . . . land in a hazard," or any one of a thousand other self-pitying premonitions.

The game of golf is hard. It puts demands upon us not only physically, but also mentally. Perhaps more so than any other sport, golf is a game in which participants often feel completely at the mercy of forces outside of their control. Certainly, there is some truth to this theory, for variables including wind, rain, excessive heat, cold, course conditions, playing partners, galleries, competition, and many other factors can wreak havoc on one's score. However, a golfer often uses the influence of one or more of these variables as an excuse. The golfer did not fail, he or she was a victim.

The existence of a "victim's mentality" is not exclusive to the golf world. In fact, it is so prevalent in our society that it is nearly at epidemic levels. Perhaps in an effort toward preservation of one's self-image, it is easier to blame the bad things that have happened to you on twists of fate, not accept them as results of some action you took or failed to take. It is simply a question of accountability.

Great champions accept accountability. If not for more noble reasons then for the simple reason that if you feel completely at the whim of circumstances that you cannot control, then how can you possibly compete? Not only are you competing against an opponent, you are also subject to the fickle injustices of millions of other variables.

I believe that there are two kinds of outcome on a golf course: an *objective event* and a *subjective event*.

An *objective event* is the reality of where your ball ends up, regardless of cause. Perhaps your perfectly hit drive hit a drainage cover or a sprinkler head, or settled in a divot. Perhaps it plugged into the bunker or rolled into an unraked footprint. Maybe it caught a tiny piece of a limb extending over the dogleg, just enough to knock it out of bounds or into a hazard. Whatever the cause, the ball is where it is and no amount of complaining or long conspiracy theories that you are "the most unlucky golfer on the earth" will change that reality.

A *subjective event* is your reaction to the facts as presented. Did you respond in a measured, prudent, logical way, or did you choose to lash out, to "get even," to immaturely display your displeasure at not "getting your way" as if you were two years old? Did you slam your club or throw it? Did you cry out in anger?

The golf history books are long on stories of how a match was decided not on the merits of who had a better swing or mastery of the fundamentals of golf, but simply because one of the competitors defeated himself through the complete loss of composure and concentration.

Failing to accept full accountability, allowing yourself to be a victim, is a reflection of the image you have of yourself and the world. You are the cause of 100 percent of everything that happens to you. Even if you are subjected to an objective event, it is your subjective response that will determine its ultimate impact on you. Everyone, in equal measure, has both "good" and "bad" luck every day. It is amazing that the golfer who does not complain or dwell on the occurrences of bad luck is assumed to not have any, while the one who bemoans his fate is assumed to have nothing but. The latter is a limiting mentality that leads to self-defeat.

The way to overcome a tendency to blame is to accept adversity as an opportunity to learn, with humility and with humor. Be honest with yourself. Is some of your bad luck caused by failure to practice a particular part of your game? Would your ball landing in a bunker really be that horrible a fate if you practiced bunker shots until you were confident and proficient about extracting the ball from the sand?

There is only one thing that we really have control over in golf or in life, and that is our response to adversity. We can practice and we can prepare for its arrival, but when it shows up, it is up to us to determine its impact. While the outcome, the objective event, may have already taken place, you are the master of your response. While this may not keep your drive from landing in the bunker or deep rough, it may just keep you from lofting the ball on your next shot over the green in an adrenaline-driven rage.

We live in a land of tremendous opportunity where we can literally become whatever we choose to make of ourselves. We are limited *only by our vision* of what we can be and our *commitment to make it happen*. With the world of abundance and opportunity we live in, the next time you are tempted to say, "With my luck . . . ," it is safe to assume your ball is going in the hole, because that is how heavily the odds are in your favor.

"I never wanted to be a millionaire. I just wanted to live like one."

᳁ Walter Hagen

11

Stand Out!

ॐ

A legend died the other day. He was irascible yet funny, tight with his money yet generous with his time. If you want to go by longevity, of being able to win when he was in his twenties or when he was in his fifties, Sam Snead was the greatest golfer of all time.

I only met Snead twice. The first time was a golf date, and I have to tell you, I was excited about it. This was seven or eight years ago, when he was already a man in his eighties. And I have to say that I was not bowled over by his pleasantries. I don't even think he said "hi" on the first tee. Somebody introduced the foursome, Snead grunted, and play began.

Not many things stand out about that day, but I do remember one thing in particular. Snead asked me if I had played the course before. Yes, I said, I've played it several times. Well, came the surprising question, how far is it to clear that bunker?

Now, this was a second shot into a green, not a tee shot. Even at his advanced age, Snead drove it 30 yards past me. I was

---

*This piece was written on May 24, 2002, only days after the passing of Sam Snead. It was written by one of the finest golf writers in the nation, George White, who writes for GolfChannel.com.

"The biggest thing is to have the mindset and belief that you can win every tournament. Nicklaus had it."

৵ Tiger Woods

dealing with a yardage I hadn't seen before. I have to say, in thirty years of playing golf, not one person has ever asked me how far it is to clear a bunker. But I made an estimate—about 160, I guessed.

Snead swung and hit the ball—and it plopped right into the middle of the bunker, sand billowing upward as the ball struck. Obviously it was 165 or 170, if he had hit it right. I'm not a pro, don't normally consider yardages to carry bunkers, and so I didn't think a lot of it. Until—he directed his full wrath at me.

"One-sixty my (posterior)!" he roared. "I thought you said you've played this course! That ball was a full ten yards short!"

I made a mental note to give no more yardages to Mr. Snead.

He settled down a hole or two later and began telling a long list of risqué jokes. Most were so old that I winced, but still snickered out of politeness. Along went the afternoon, until we were on about the fifteenth green.

Sam had a three-foot putt. He carefully lined it up, stroked it—and missed.

He turned around. He leaped into the air. He twisted once or twice, then began a self-directed tirade: "You no-good, no-hustle, no-putting (expletive deleted, expletive deleted, expletive deleted)." He was turning the air various shades of red, blue, and green with his language. And then it hit me.

Sam was very serious about his golf. This was a charity match, it meant absolutely nothing. Sam's fee had already been paid by—whoever. He had done thousands upon thousands of these exercises. But he was STILL a grinder, still trying, still adamant when he missed. And here was a man in his eighties. Suddenly, his outburst that was directed toward me earlier in the round made so much sense.

The second time we met, Sam was considerably more pleasant. I had gone to his house in Fort Pierce, Florida, to do a story for the Golf Channel. Sam was extremely cheerful. Golf wasn't involved, of course, and he was free to just ramble.

"The first thing anybody has to do to be any good at anything is believe in himself."

∽ Gay Brewer

And ramble. And ramble. I had a tape recorder with me, and it was running the whole two hours. The conversation was liberally sprinkled with curse words and off-color jokes. The jokes were old, many of them were repeats of the jokes I'd heard playing golf with Sam a couple of years before, jokes that I'd heard many times before that.

Afterward, I mentioned to an aide of Snead's that I had taped the conversation, that there was no need for concern that some of the quotes might be wrong. The aide shrank back in horror, blanching at the prospect of hearing Ol' Sam totally unplugged.

"No, no," he stammered. "Don't use that tape! Don't use those curse words!"

I carefully reassured the gentleman that the tape was not going to be used verbatim.

Sam, incidentally, didn't mind what he said, or what we used. But one thing he said really stuck with me. I asked him about Hogan, about Sarazen, about Nelson, information about each of them to be used for future pieces, perhaps obituaries.

Anyway, Snead gave a little speech about each one. I know a lot of the clatter was bogus, but who cares? It was good theater.

Then he leaned back and said, "You know, there is a time for all of us to go home."

No cussing, no jokes, no off-color stories this time—just an elderly gentleman talking for a moment about something extremely personal. Now the time has finally come. Sam Snead has gone home.

"Management, placing the ball in the right position for the next shot, is eighty percent of winning golf."

᠆ Ben Hogan

Be Distinctive

Golf's greats were all distinctive:

Old Tom Morris was the humble father of golf.
Vardon was the first great star.
Donald Ross was golf's Michelangelo.
Ouimet was a pioneer.
Hagen was flamboyant.
Zaharias was complete.
Jones was supremely gifted.
Snead was a natural athlete.
Hogan was a master of control.
Palmer transcended the game.
Player was determined.
Thompson was balanced.
Nicklaus was focused power.
Trevino was tenacious.
Miller was a shooting star.
Watson was fearless.
Lopez was unstoppable.
Ballesteros was dashing.
Faldo was highly disciplined.
Woods is a power artist.
Sorenstam is precise.

The variety of styles and diversity of strengths are part of what makes their legends so much fun.

It is important that we should strive to make ourselves distinctive as well. We must establish ourselves as unique authorities and experts in our field of choice. We simply cannot stand out when we are buried in the pack. Becoming distinctive, an expert authority, gives you credibility and the ability to use your forum as a basis of expansion into other areas where you have a passion and a desire to learn.

You may not be the longest driver of the ball, but at what aspect of the game can you work so hard that you can gain above-average proficiency? How about your short game? Putting and chipping are universally maligned for their difficulty and the critical role they play in the execution of a well-played round. Yet they require no particular area of physical dominance such as great size, strength, or athletic ability. Mastery of the short game is a choice. Like any area in life where we desire to break out of the pack, it requires a commitment to be as good as we can possibly be. This may require lessons, research, reading, and endlessly practicing fundamentals and techniques. Most important it requires the one thing that derails most people from the path of reaching their goals: it requires disciplined tenacity.

While we should seek to distinguish ourselves in all aspects of our lives, one particular area of importance is at our place of employment. The sad reality is that at most businesses today, there exists an undercurrent of insecurity that slowly erodes company morale and motivation with its harsh abrasions. If you work at a job with an environment where it is commonplace that people tear one another apart through rumors, gossip, character assassination, meanness, and lack of cooperation, then you can distinguish yourself by making a decision to stop playing that game. You will stand out by moving in the opposite direction. Go out of your way to celebrate others' successes. Be willing to give credit to others (even if most of it belongs to you). An effective way to do this is with interoffice e-mail. It is important to use positive, affirming language when you address your peers and even your supervisors. It is particularly important to maintain this disposition in private settings, for over time this is how you build trust. If those you come into contact with trust that you will not speak negatively about them when they are not present, then eventually they will afford you the same courtesy.

Poor managers attempt to manage through intimidation and instilling insecurity. They need to feel that the business is exploiting the employees; getting more out of the employees than they are being given. Their business environments are devoid of support, nurturing, and empowerment. Unfortunately, the necessity of exploitation is a basic, but misguided, belief of unenlightened managers. The beauty of distinguishing yourself as a force for positive energy in your office has multiple benefits. First, it is infectious and marks you as a leader. Next, most managers have no idea how to manage you! You start to appear as though everything you touch turns to gold. Your boss comes to the conclusion that you are either extremely lucky or bring out the best in everyone around you (and he is right on both counts). You become the model employee, yet you have done it by being supportive and reaching out to your fellow employees.

Being distinctive does not happen by accident. We need to decide how we wish to be defined, whether on the golf course, at home, at school, or at our place of employment.

Being distinctive takes the courage not to be afraid to stand alone. None of the game's great players were afraid to stand alone, for it was what they did every time they hoisted the champion's trophy.

"Don't give advice unless you are asked."

~ Amy Alcott

"Practice is the only golf advice that is good for everybody."

~ Arnold Palmer

12

Surround Yourself with Experts

ॐ

HALF IN THE BOTTLE

Surely, Harry Bradshaw would not be the first golfer to see his championship hopes dashed by the devastating impact of a bottle. Only in his case, it was quite literal.

After an opening-round 68, the Irish golfer was contending for the Open Championship at Royal St. George's when, during the second round, his tee shot on the fifth hole flew into the semi-rough, settling into the bottom half of a broken beer bottle.

Unlike today's tournaments, where it is fairly easy to beckon a tournament official for a ruling, in 1949 rules officials were not instantly available. Rather than hail an official, and await their arrival and then their decision, Bradshaw decided to take matters into his own hands.

Choosing a sand wedge and closing his eyes as tightly as he could, Bradshaw took a mighty swing at the brown glass–encased ball, resulting in a shower of glass splinters and advancing the ball some thirty yards. Now laying two, Bradshaw seemed unnerved by the incident and proceeded to record a six on the hole.

He would finish with a 77 for the day and follow that up with rounds of 68 and 70 to finish in a tie with South African Bobby Locke. In the 36-hole play-off, Bradshaw was soundly defeated by Locke, 135 to 147.

Bradshaw would later admit that he had no idea whether he

was entitled to take relief from the bottle, and his actions clearly indicated that he had no interest in consulting with an expert who might have ruled in his favor. While this latter point has been hotly debated as to the ambiguity of the governing rule at that time (which was shortly thereafter clarified) and as to whether relief would have been granted, one thing is for sure, without at least asking for a ruling, no one will ever know whether a ruling would have been made in his favor.

Bradshaw's ball coming to rest in a broken bottle was a cruel twist of fate. However, whether it was due to nerves or a poorly defined rule, Bradshaw chose to act without consulting an expert and had to live with the results of his actions. Those actions may have cost him the 1949 Open Championship.

᠅

A Road to Failure

The famed bunkers on the Old Course at St. Andrews have swallowed up many championship aspirations over their long history—perhaps none more tragically than those of poor David Ayton at the 1885 Open Championship.

Ayton arrived at the seventy-first hole of the championship with a commanding five-stroke lead over Bob Martin. Few could have possibly doubted that Ayton would close out the round as the champion. This point of view was bolstered by Ayton's drive on the seventeenth hole in the middle of the fairway and by an approach shot to the green that fell just short of its mark, but in a relatively easy position from which to pitch onto the putting surface.

Surely Ayton's steps were light as he surveyed his very manageable situation and entertained thoughts of becoming the reigning Open champion and with that, the finest golfer in the world.

Perhaps it is at times like these that we need a strong voice of reason to rein us in and remind us to finish the job at hand before casting our minds to the rewards for an accomplishment not yet earned.

Ayton's first attempt to pitch the ball was underhit, and his ball veered off the green, dribbling down into the unforgiving Road Hole bunker that protects the front of the putting surface. Ayton corrected his prior error of hitting the ball too weakly, but this time he used too much muscle. His ball sailed from the bunker and over the green, settling on the road that encircles the back of the green. Then his troubles really began. His first chip was played too soft, hitting the banking on the front of the green and rolling back at him onto the road surface. His next attempt was too firmly struck, and the ball raced through the green and dove back into the same bunker where it had come from just minutes before. This time, Ayton's determination to hit the bunker shot perfectly, so as to hold the green, resulted in a compounding of errors, and it took him three shots to extricate his ball. Once on the green, Ayton two-putted to record a score of 11 on the hole.

Ayton's misfortune would drop him into third place, two shots behind the winner, Bob Martin.

゛プ

Surround Yourself with Experts

Part of the appeal of golf is the inherent wisdom that is fundamental to the game. Take for example, Rule 8–1, from the Rules of Golf, that prohibits a player from:

a) *Give[giving] advice to anyone in the competition playing on the course other than his partner, or*

b) *ask[ing] for advice from anyone other than his partner or either of their caddies.*

Can you imagine how helpful this rule would be if we could carry it beyond the confines of the golf course?

Why, the next time some know-it-all begins to advise us how "unrealistic" we are being in the pursuit of our goals by not settling for a normal, boring, uninspiring existence, we can simply hold up our hand and say, "Sorry, Rule 8–1."

The world is full of people who believe that they are helping us by sharing their opinions of how we should be living. My friends who are PGA teaching professionals will often chuckle listening to one high-handicap golfer giving swing advice to another, for it is usually wrong. The cost of lost golf balls alone should be enough to motivate these golfers to seek out an expert opinion.

However, the world is full of people and information that would be helpful in the pursuit of our goals. The key is seeking out the ones who really know and then being willing to listen.

Many amateur golfers would never think of visiting a golf instructor. When you think about it, that's like a person with a persistent cough who never goes to the doctor. The most common excuse for not visiting a PGA instructor is that the golfer is afraid

"Don't analyze your own swing. The chances are you can't do it properly. Have a pro do the job."

↝ Sam Snead

of going through the period when a swing gets broken down and then rebuilt. Most would rather live with marginal mediocrity, usually in the form of a weak slice, then face the prospect of change.

Ironically, there is hardly a great player in the world today that does not regularly consult with not only a golf instructor, but usually also a sports psychologist, nutritionist, personal trainer, manager, and others.

When I was working on my first NASCAR book (*Chicken Soup for the NASCAR Soul*), I worked on a story with Michael Waltrip, past champion of the Daytona 500. Although it is easy to make the assumption that NASCAR racing is principally about the skill and tenacity of the driver, each NASCAR team, including Michael's, has a deep stable of talent. In today's racing, it is not unusual to have over one hundred people on a racing team's staff, each with specific areas of expertise. While interviewing Michael about the importance of utilizing experts, he said something to me that I will never forget. "Life is a team sport," Michael said. This simple wisdom has profound insight.

We do not need to face life's challenges alone. Family, loved ones, and friends are all valuable sources of support. In many of the more complex areas of our lives there are countless experts available to us to help make our journey a little easier. Getting help from an expert is not a sign of weakness. On the contrary, it is the sign of someone who is open to the highest levels of learning and accomplishment.

While experts can assist us in many aspects of life, it is helpful to identify a sole individual, a *mentor*, to guide us down our primary path. A mentor can be a coach, a parent, a teacher, a professional, or someone we do not even know, yet in each case we aspire to follow the mentor's path. In fact, the best way to identify a person you wish to be your mentor is to study the method the person used to succeed. Chances are that person had a mentor as well. In choosing a mentor it is sometimes best to reach as high as you can, outside your comfort zone, and ask someone you perceive to be well above your level to be your

"Practice is not to take the place of teaching, but to make teaching worthwhile.

～ Harvey Penick

mentor. Mentoring can take as little as a brief phone call each week or a regular exchange of e-mails. You will be surprised how many highly accomplished people are willing to mentor those who have the courage to *ask*.

Oftentimes the mentor gets as much out of the experience as you do. Not only does the mentor feel good helping another, but mentoring also helps to reiterate the principles and work ethic that helped the mentor succeed and might even provide a reminder of some that he or she had let slip.

Having a mentor is also an excellent way to start networking and getting to know the right people.

The game of golf has demonstrated its infinite wisdom in Rule 8–1, which protects us from bad, or at the very least, competitively biased advice. The game also embraces and promotes the importance of the Professional Golfers Association of America as a source of experts who can assist us with the game's more challenging aspects.

We should all be open and willing to listen to the advice of experts. Combining that posture with getting a mentor could be our smartest career decision on or off the course.

"When you go head to head against Nicklaus, he knows he's going to beat you, you know he's going to beat you, and he knows you know he's going to beat you."

～ J. C. SNEAD

13

Major Goals

༄

NOTHING TO LOSE

Sometimes the fastest way to reach our major goals is to realize we have nothing to lose in making the effort.

Such was the case with an unpredictable Tour rookie named John Daly at the 1991 PGA Championship. Daly had missed eleven of twenty-four cuts coming into the tournament, as well as missing the cut in sectional qualifying for the PGA.

Less than a day before the tournament, Daly was mired in the position of ninth alternate. Slowly players began to drop out until Daly was just one player from making the event.

Knowing that his chances were now looking good to get in, Daly set out on the seven-plus-hour drive from his home in Arkansas to the Crooked Stick golf course outside Indianapolis. By the time he checked into his hotel room, after midnight, the blinking message light on his room's phone shone like a beacon of opportunity, as his position in the tournament was secured when Nick Price dropped out due to the birth of his first child.

Daly would retain the caddieing services of Price's caddie, Squeeky Medlen, which was one more twist of fate that paved Daly's path to the improbable.

Daly shocked the golf world with an opening round 69 on a course he had never seen before, without the benefit of practice. He stood just two shots out of the lead. Even more shocking was

"I just came here to play golf and got lucky."

~ John Daly, 1991
PGA champion

when he fired a second-round 67 and led the tournament by a stroke over Bruce Lietzke at the halfway point.

Daly's ability to drive the golf ball massive distances is well known today, but in 1991 he was like a circus act. Medlen wisely encouraged Daly to exploit his strengths and play his game by advising him to "Grip it and rip it!" This approach overpowered the golf course and the rest of the field. Daly's prodigious drives also overshadowed a very solid short game that delivered every time he needed it.

Daly would shoot rounds of 69 and 70 on Saturday and Sunday to secure not only his first victory on the PGA Tour, but a major tournament, no less (Daly would win another major tournament at the 1995 Open Championship at St. Andrews).

"I came to the tournament with nothing to lose," Daly would say, "and that had everything to do with winning."

"Focus not on the commotion around you, but on the opportunity ahead of you."

ᡣ Arnold Palmer

~

Major Goals—Thinking Big

When Tiger Woods was a kid he had Jack Nicklaus' impressive achievements taped to his wall as motivation. Even for a golf prodigy like Woods, Nicklaus' golfing accomplishments read like something superhuman that only a fool or someone severely self-deluded would even aspire to. But Tiger Woods was different. He did not use Nicklaus' record as an opportunity to take account of his deficiencies, but as a road map to success—as a cause of self-empowerment, not resignation.

Consider the list that would greet a young Tiger Woods each day as he awoke and glanced up at the faded paper taped to the wall.

Jack Nicklaus' Golfing Record
2—U.S. Amateurs ('59, '61)
1—NCAA Championship ('61)
6—Masters Championships ('63, '65, '66, '72, '75, '86)
4—U.S. Opens ('62, '67, '72, '80)
3—Open Championships ('66, '70, '78)
5—PGA Championships ('63, '71, '73, '75, '80)

In addition to this, Nicklaus finished in the top three in majors forty-eight times, including nineteen second-place finishes, nine third-place finishes, fifty-six top-five finishes, and seventy-three top-ten finishes. Nicklaus also won the Players Championship (increasingly referred to as the "fifth major") three times, and the Australian Open six times. His seventy-three victories on the PGA Tour are second only to Sam Snead on the all-time list.

"You win major tournaments with your mind."

～ Tiger Woods

Whether Tiger Woods will overtake Nicklaus in any or all of these categories is irrelevant. The important point is that Woods realized that to accomplish great things you first have to believe yourself capable of it. You have to train yourself to thinking big.

Thinking big helps us see a world of opportunity that may have previously been just outside our range of sight. It allows us to look to the possibilities on the horizon without having the view obscured by perceived obstacles that stand between us and our wildest dreams. Thinking big is not only fun; it is critical to success.

Thinking big is a developed trait. We can train ourselves to embrace the possibilities without giving in to limiting self-doubt. The chief inhibitor to thinking big, to going for it, is fear. Fear of failure. Fear of rejection. Fear of ridicule for trying something over our heads. I love the mantra of author Raymond Aaron, who encourages his students to "Bite off more than you can chew and chew like crazy."

The funny thing is that as I travel and meet with immensely successful people in all fields, every one of them has admitted to intense fear. Their fear occurred at the same times and places as we would feel it if we were in the same position. Perhaps it was a first job, or management position. Maybe one was about to ask the love of his life to marry him, or about to become a parent for the first time. Perhaps another was standing on the first tee on the final day of a major, in the last group. But they all fought through the fear. They rejected it and focused solely on their dreams. They used their big thinking to fill their minds with nothing but their dreams. They did not have room for doubt. They greeted insecurity with intensity of purpose. Of course, after they succeeded, they were met with a chorus of supporters who "knew they had it in them." The reality is that early on, many high achievers simply kept their huge aspirations to themselves rather than face the ridicule of others who were satisfied with mediocrity. Often, you are the only one who knows what your potential really is. The challenge is to have the courage to follow

"The difference between winning and losing is always a mental one."

༝ Peter Thompson

your conviction and embrace the possibilities regardless of internal or external pressure to settle for less.

The irony of thinking big is that it takes just as much effort as thinking small. The top-producing salespeople in any field will admit that it takes just as much effort to ask for a million-dollar order as it does a $10,000 order. For my part, it takes as much effort to produce, write, and host a feature that is broadcast around the world on The Golf Channel as it would to do it for a local cable access channel. It helps to have a "national" mentality when setting your sights. If it takes the same amount of time and effort, why not go big-time?

Big thinkers are usually excellent negotiators because they shoot for the sky. They know that it is always easier to come down on a price or service than to negotiate your way up. My friend, who is a power lifter, likes to quote a line he heard as a child in a cartoon that said, "Think big and be big." Big thinkers really do think this way. They do not prequalify themselves as being too small, too inexperienced, too young, too late, or not ready. They take the chance without reservation. They let everyone else convince themselves that they are not ready for the challenge, thus diminishing the competitive field.

Big thinkers are busy looking forward while everyone else is looking backward. They define their self-images by what they will be, not what they are, or have been. Detractors dismiss them as "dreamers." In fact, dreamers are exactly what they are. They know that if you do not have the courage to dream big then you will never accomplish big things.

Now is a good time to decide what list of unrestricted accomplishments we wish to aspire to. Review every goal you have established in your life personally and professionally and start thinking really, really big. Resist the temptation to edit how high you should aspire. Take the highest vision you have of your goals and multiply them by ten.

Write down your goals, tape the list on the wall, and use it as your guide, every day. Remember that the bigger your dreams, the bigger your accomplishments. Tiger did.

*"Fear of any kind is the number-one enemy
of all golfers, regardless of ball-striking
and shot-making capabilities."*

∽ Jack Nicklaus

14

One-Up Fear

ぶ

A FIGHTING SPIRIT

One golfer who could definitely use his life experiences as a source of strength to overcome fear and pressure was Bobby Cruickshank.

Cruickshank enjoyed more than a decade of prominence in professional golf during the 1920s and 1930s. Cruickshank was a tough competitor; that can be said without debate.

In World War I, the Scottish-born Cruickshank served as a British soldier. During the war he had the misfortune to witness his own brother's death as he was ripped to pieces by a German shell. Later, Cruickshank was captured and sent to a German POW camp. He escaped, fighting his way through enemy lines to rejoin British forces.

To illustrate how tough he was, Cruickshank is remembered for a self-inflicted blow to the head during the 1934 U.S. Open. In the third round, while leading the tournament, a wayward second shot on the eleventh hole hit a rock in a streambed and then ricocheted onto the green. Cruickshank declared "Thank you, Lord!" and tossed his club into the air in celebration. Unfortunately, the Lord's good graces and the forces of gravity were not swayed by his enthusiasm, and the club came crashing back down to the earth, striking Cruickshank squarely on the head and knocking him to the ground. Cruickshank was paired with Wiffy Cox, who

"Fear comes in two packages, fear of failure, and sometimes fear of success."

~ Tom Kite

after checking on Cruickshank and finding the club did little visible damage to his skull, nearly joined Cruickshank on the ground due to being doubled over with laughter. For his part, the determined Cruickshank would play through the discomfort of his injury to finish the tournament (the tournament was eventually won by Olin Dutra by one stroke over Gene Sarazen).

Cruickshank's tenure as a professional golfer happened to match up with the golden age of golf, and he annually went into battle with the likes of Bobby Jones and Gene Sarazen, among others. He would finish his career having reached the finals in the 1922 and 1923 PGA Championship (losing both times to Sarazen) and the 1923 and 1932 U.S. Opens (losing to Jones and Sarazen, respectively). In a testament to his fortitude, during the 1932 PGA Championship in a match with Al Watrous, Cruickshank came back in sudden death from being nine down with twelve holes to play.

"When you're playing for $500 and you have to borrow a penny to spot your ball, now that's pressure."

↬ Lee Trevino

꒰꩜꒱

One Up on Fear

Fear has a place in golf that is as old as the game itself. Fear *is* the challenge from within that represents the quintessential essence of golf. Beyond all others, including weather, terrain, and competition, it is the psychological match play in our minds that represents golf's greatest challenge. It is the fear raging in every golfer's mind that a glimpse of his or her human frailty and true self-image will be revealed. We are petrified that our insecurities will be played out for the world to see. We cannot hide; we are alone, dependent upon ourselves, and it is scary.

Fear is a particularly insidious adversary because it attempts to strip us of our confidence and trust. Fears of failure (of every variety), embarrassment, and ridicule number among its forces.

Conquering fear entails understanding what it is. Fears are *created* in the mind. Fear is based upon the anticipation of danger. It is a forecast of an adverse future event. We literally frighten ourselves into believing that the mind's fiction is reality. Racing heart, rising blood pressure, and a splintering focus lead to tension and anxiety, the last things we need in order to perform to our optimum level.

To beat fear we need to remove its credibility. Our fears lie to us. We need to concentrate on the here and now, the challenge we face, the shot before us. We must stay focused in the present and concentrate on our plans.

Golf is unique in that persons with great success in other areas of life become irrationally paralyzed with fear at the prospect of hitting a little white stationary ball into a distant hole.

I believe that you can use your life's successes as a means

"One always feels that he is running from something without knowing what nor where it is."

～ Bobby Jones,
   on pressure in
   Majors

to minimize fear's impact. To do this you need to replace your fears with confidence and conviction you carry from some other aspect of your life. What are you so good at that you feel you are among the best, you are "world class"? What accomplishments, triumphs, and convictions are you willing to measure against those of anyone else in the world? Are you a world-class sales-person, professional, manager, analyst, or executive? Do you feel that you are the world's best father or mother, coach, teacher, or volunteer? Have you ever carried yourself, your family, or loved ones through a tragedy, sickness, or surgery? Surely if you can persevere through this, you can handle an up-and-down to save par or a double-breaking putt to close out a match?

Overcoming fear in golf is having the courage to replace fear, insecurity, and anxiety with the same tested confidence and swagger you carry in other parts of your life. Courage is not oblivious to fear; it simply stands up to it with the knowledge that playing a game is nothing compared to the battles you have fought, and won, in other aspects of life.

Often it is the ability to deal with the fear of failure that defines the difference between a champion and an also-ran. Champions know that failure is inevitable. It is impossible to perform per-fectly 100 percent of the time. What is important is whether we learn from the failure. Otherwise we are doomed to repeat it.

We need to insure that we do not waste the opportunity that failure gives us to learn from the experience. We should fully understand it. It helps to write it down in detail. Look for a recur-ring theme, action, or decision. Boil it down to a trigger point. Be as specific as possible. It is important that we are honest with ourselves in our assessments.

Losers see failure as an ending. Champions see failure as a new beginning.

It is important that we continue to remind ourselves that we are *winners*. Winners use failure as a building block to improve, to get stronger.

The next time fear tries to launch an assault, remind yourself

"Losers see failure as an ending. Champions see failure as a new beginning."

of who you are, where you have been, and what you have been through. Make a mental commitment to face the challenge at hand with the same conviction, courage, and determination as you have used to overcome obstacles of far greater meaning.

"This is the essence of strategic architecture: to encourage initiative, reward a well-played stroke, and yet to insist that there must be planning and honest self-appraisal behind the daring."

~ Robert Trent Jones Sr.

15

Overcoming Obstacles

৵

A COLLISION WITH FATE

Ben Hogan won ten times in 1948 and demonstrated a mastery over full post war fields that defined his legend.

The year 1949 began in equally promising fashion as he won the Long Beach Open in a play-off and finished second the next week, after losing in a play-off, at the Arizona Open. Both the play-off victory and loss were to his friend Jimmy Demaret.

Deciding that they needed a little time off, Ben and Valerie Hogan climbed into their black Cadillac and set off for their new Texas home. Ben Hogan was driving when a heavy fog descended like a thick blanket upon the west Texas highway. Hogan reduced his speed to a crawl. While they were crossing a cement-lined bridge, a Greyhound bus that was passing a truck suddenly pulled into the Hogans' lane without any possibility of avoiding a collision. Hogan jerked his car to the right as far as he could. "Honey, he's going to hit us!" screamed Valerie seconds before the nearly 20,000-pound bus hit them head-on on the driver's side.

Ben Hogan's love and devotion to his beloved wife Valerie has never been in question, and he demonstrated his selfless commitment to her by throwing his body across her a mere fraction of a second before the crash. Hogan's act undoubtedly saved his wife from being thrown through the windshield, and she escaped

"Wind and rain are great challenges. They separate the real golfers. Let the seas pound against the shore, let the rain pour."

∾ Tom Watson

with minor injuries. Hogan likely saved his own life as well, as the force of the crash drove the steering wheel through the driver's side seat. However, Hogan's legs were still on the car's crushed left side, where the engine now stood. His legs were badly injured. It took an hour to extract the Hogans from the mangled wreckage. In total, Hogan sustained a broken collarbone, a smashed rib, a broken ankle, a double fracture of the pelvis, bladder injuries, and deep contusions to his left leg.

Hogan was rushed to an El Paso hospital where doctors feared the legend would not live, and that if he did, he might never walk again. Hogan developed blood clots that reached his lungs. The doctors performed abdominal surgery and tied off the main vein to his leg to prevent further blood clots from reaching his heart. A second clot was discovered, and Hogan was operated on again.

Hogan would slowly recover from his devastating injuries, although it would take more than eleven months before he could make it back to a golf tournament.

As tenacious a competitor as Hogan is remembered as being, nothing he ever did with a golf club compares to his heroic determination to regain his championship form.

Hogan would return to the Tour in 1950 at the Los Angeles Open and would, remarkably, take Sam Snead into a play-off, which Snead eventually won, in his first tournament back. But Hogan would never again be as strong as he was before the accident. Hogan's legs would ache after each tournament, and he decided to concentrate his efforts on golf's Major tournaments.

Needing to soak his legs after every round and playing golf with his legs wrapped in Ace bandages, Hogan faced his greatest obstacle at the 1950 U.S. Open, which at that time required thirty-six holes of golf on the final day.

It was a mere sixteen months after his horrific accident when Hogan hit his most famous shot. He hit a perfect 1-iron on the eighteenth hole at Merion that set up a par and secured his position in a play-off the next day with Lloyd Mangrum and George Fazio. Hogan would shoot a 69 during the play-off to secure the

"Laddie, a blind hole is blind only once to a man with a memory."

∽ Tommy Armour

"Golf is a job to me. I love to play, but I'm very serious about what I do."

∽ Vijay Singh

victory (interestingly, he would do it without the 1-iron he used the day before—the club was stolen the night before the play-off and not returned to Hogan for thirty-six years).

Hogan would go on to win six Majors after the accident and a total of nine for his career.

Ben Hogan's record, particularly in majors, is among the best the game has ever known. However, when viewed from the perspective of what he had to overcome to achieve it, it becomes clear why Hogan is the game's greatest icon.

"One might as well attempt to describe the smoothness of the wind as to paint a clear picture of his complete swing."

~ Grantland Rice, on Bobby Jones

"Put him three strokes behind anybody, and he believes he's the favorite."

~ Frank Beard, on Arnold Palmer

How Long Is This Hole?

Golf course architects have a few tricks that they like to employ to make a golf hole seem much more ominous. One such trick is to build up the green complex so that the top of the green seems almost suspended in air. Usually, the green is surrounded by broad, sloping hills that keep trees and vegetation a considerable distance away from the putting surface. The result is the illusion that the green is farther away from the golfer than it actually is because the eye lacks a reference near the green from which to ascertain distance. Combine this with a narrow shoot at the tee box, a bunker placed around 400 yards from the tee (to draw the eye), and some gentle mounding to define the contours of the hole, and a hole measuring around 425 yards (while not short, certainly not a monster by today's standards) seems like it is 800 yards long. A particular master at visual deception was the course architect genius Donald Ross. While most of his courses were not designed to be very long compared to modern courses, he could make a 325-yard hole seem three times as large. When you recall that his courses existed before the advent of yardage books and GPS systems, it gives an even greater appreciation for his mastery. If the mark of a classic is the way it stands the test of time, then Ross' Pinehurst No. 2 pretty much says it all.

The bottom line is that Ross and others like him provide us with the opportunity to create an obstacle in our minds that is bigger than it is in reality.

Overcoming obstacles represents the very foundation of golf. Each shot carries with it a new challenge: a new set of variables to contend with such as wind, slope of the landing area, width of the fairway, the size and shape of the green, and the pin position, among others. Of course, while the physical demand of execut-

"He was the most dedicated practitioner of all time. His tenacity had no equal."

↬ Paul Runyan, on Ben Hogan

"Sam Snead is one of a handful of golfers who inspire the club players with the conviction that golf is easy."

↬ Peter Dobereiner

ing the shots necessary to overcome these obstacles is challenging, what can be even more formidable is the mental strain they cause. This is compounded by pressure from competition, stress, and anxiety over execution.

In an effort to illustrate the steps necessary to overcome the obstacles we may face in life, this chapter uses character traits of some of the game's greatest champions as examples from which to draw inspiration. Here are the steps to execute.

Have the vision of Nicklaus: Overcoming obstacles requires vision. Vision allows us to see the possibilities that exist on the horizon, beyond the fog of adversity that surrounds us.

No player in the history of the game had better vision than Jack Nicklaus. Nicklaus had the career vision to prepare his game for the major championships, ignoring the critics who claimed he did not play in enough weekly Tour events. While Nicklaus has a very impressive record in non-majors, he understood that great players are judged by their performance in Majors. Nicklaus' vision led to a plan to be prepared for the Masters, U.S. Open, The Open Championship, and the PGA Championship before all others.

Have the perspective of Jones: Bobby Jones' pursuit of the Grand Slam in 1930 was wrought with tribulation. The fact that Jones accomplished this amazing feat is staggering, especially given the fact that he was an amateur golfer, and, contrary to the popular misconception, was not independently wealthy, so he had to contend with the everyday struggles of life just like the rest of us. In addition, the pressures of expectation were enormous not only because he was a golf prodigy, but also because with each victory the excitement and anticipation grew (especially in America, which was struggling with the Depression and desperately needed a hero). Jones also faced fiercely tough competition from golfers eager for the fame of having stopped his march into the history books. Add to all the challenges the fact that he was not at the top of his game through some of this stretch (understandably so), and the monumental stature of his accomplishment starts to come into focus.

"Trevino has more lines than the L & N Railroad."

～ Fuzzy Zoeller

Jones persevered and triumphed because he maintained a Zen-like stoicism that allowed him to stay focused on his core strengths regardless of the tempest that whirled around him.

Have the experience of Hogan: Ben Hogan worked for every ounce of success he enjoyed. The legendary Hogan that is most remembered is the dominating golfer he became after the Second World War until the mid-1950s. Few today recall that during his early years on Tour, Hogan was broke, more than once, and he was nearly forced to give up the pursuit of his dream to be a touring professional. So desperate was Hogan as a young professional that one time he reportedly stripped an orange tree, which was adjacent to the course, of all of its fruit so that he and his wife could live on the oranges for the following two weeks.

Hogan knew that steel is hardened through fire, and he admitted that without experiencing the hard times he never would have known the great times.

Have the humor of Trevino: Lee Trevino used humor to deflect stress and anxiety.

Humor allows us to laugh at our mistakes. Humor flushes out blinding rage and negative thinking. Without the benefit of humor, our anger only compounds our problems.

Of course Trevino had great confidence in his ability. Humor does not diminish conviction or minimize that fact that a mistake has been made. Humor simply allows us to adjust faster and not dwell on what is in the past.

Have the helping spirit of Penick: When the legendary golf instructor Harvey Penick died in 1995 at the age of ninety, he left behind a legacy that went beyond that of just a great teacher of the game. Penick, whose students included Ben Crenshaw and Tom Kite, taught the game in a way that revealed as much about life as about golf. What's more, Penick did it in a manner that both showed great respect for his students and left an indelible mark, through masterly and economical use of words. He did this by ingeniously leading his pupils down the path of their own discoveries rather than forcing them to learn by submission.

"*A golf course is to me holy ground. I feel God in the trees, and the grass and flowers, and in the rabbits and the birds and the squirrels; in the sky and the water. I feel that I am home.*"

᠊ᢣᠵ Harvey Penick,
from *A Game for a Lifetime*

Harvey Penick individually provided the help that his students needed. Help is all around us as well. However, we have to be willing to take advantage of it. We need to put aside our fear of rejection and embarrassment and ask for the help we need.

Have the work ethic of Vijay Singh: Being the first to arrive and the last to leave is more than just a cliché for Vijay Singh.

Singh's humble origins and ascent to the top of the world of golf are a testament to the rewards that await those who approach any task with an unrelenting tenacity. No one works harder, or longer, on his or her game than Vijay Singh, and the results speak for themselves.

Have the commitment of Snead: Sam Snead was unrelenting in his pursuit of golfing excellence. The fact that Snead was one of the most naturally gifted athletes to ever play the game sometimes obscures the fact of how precisely committed he was to his craft.

Snead owns the record for the most all-time PGA Tour victories with 82, but his burning passion for the game was also demonstrated by his longevity at its highest ranks. He played competitively on tour well past his fiftieth birthday (the Champions Tour did not begin until 1980, when Snead was already sixty-eight years old). In fact, Snead holds the record as the oldest player to make a cut on the PGA Tour. He was sixty-seven years old when he made the cut at the 1979 Manufacturers Hanover Westchester Classic. That same year, Snead became the first player to shoot his age on tour when he posted a 67 in the second round of the 1979 Quad Cities Open.

Have the confidence of Palmer: There has never been a golfer who has rivaled Arnold Palmer for the sheer excitement he generated on the golf course. Palmer was a power golfer who could bring a golf course to its knees through his skill and through the confidence to take chances that others did not possess the stomach to even attempt.

There is no doubt that confidence is built through success, but

"I've got to continue down the path and continue working hard. I want to get to a better level, a higher level, and be more consistent day in and day out. It's as simple as that."

ᔥ Tiger Woods

it can also be built through having the courage to try the very thing that all around you would advise against.

Have the discipline of Woods: Tiger Woods possesses the physical discipline of Gary Player through his exercise program and strict nutritional plan. He possesses the consistency of Byron Nelson, having eclipsed Nelson's record of consecutive cuts made. Woods' run at consecutive cuts made would extend to 142 events (ironically, the cuts-made streak ended at the 2005 Byron Nelson Classic). He possesses the vision of Nicklaus and the confidence of Palmer.

Tiger Woods, through hard work, a plan, and courage (he *twice* retooled his Major-winning swing) has reached the highest levels of the game. His commitment and discipline serve as an example to all of us of the possibilities of what can be achieved when you are not willing to let anything stand in the way of you and your dreams.

Modern golf course architecture has changed dramatically over the last three decades, in both length and design. However, there is no hazard, no obstacle, that can be incorporated into a golf course's design that the combination of the skills listed above cannot overcome.

"In golf, as in life, you get out of it what you put into it."

৵ Sam Snead

16

An Option for How to Play It

⌇

THE RED CADILLAC

One of my favorite pictues in golf was not taken on the golf course. It is a photo from 1973, taken in the parking lot in front of the Augusta National clubhouse. In the photo, a debonair Arnold Palmer, wearing his "green jacket," is leaning back against a yacht-like, red, convertible, two-door Cadillac.

While Mr. Palmer's record speaks for itself, the photo screams of success. His totally casual pose, bringing to mind James Dean, and his satisfied smile shine like a beacon, illuminating the joy of accomplishment and of reaping the rewards for what you have achieved.

Arnold Palmer is the epitome of success in professional golf. Not only is his record on the course remarkable, but he has been blessed with the talent to translate his trusting, amiable personality into a myriad of endorsement deals over the years. In fact, his enigmatic personality and go-for-broke style of play are largely responsible for the massive expansion of professional golf. He was a mega-superstar at the same time as the professional game was being introduced to the power of television, and he was the perfect leading man.

From his humble beginnings in Latrobe, Pennsylvania, to his years of skyrocketing popularity, Mr. Palmer has made it all look so natural, so effortless. The fact is that it was not effortless.

"The most rewarding things you do in life are often the ones that look like they can't be done."

୬ Arnold Palmer

He started out as a paint salesman, and his path was filled with tremendous hard work, sacrifice, and risk. He faced self-doubt and criticism just like everyone else, but he would not let them defeat him.

In 1954, the Wilson Sporting Goods Company sent Gene Sarazen to check out the game of Arnold Palmer while he was competing in the U.S. Amateur. Sarazen reported back that the young Palmer "lunged" at the ball, and that the only shots he played were hooks. "I told Wilson the kid would never amount to much," Sarazen concluded.

Gene Sarazen was not the first person to underestimate Arnold Palmer. Palmer's indomitable spirit and tenacity are well represented in his seven-shot, come-from-behind victory in the 1960 U.S. Open at Cherry Hills. Prior to the final round, journalist Bob Drum asserted that Palmer had blown his chances in the championship with such a large deficit. It would appear that the best way to motivate Palmer is to tell him he is incapable of doing something, for he proceeded to start the round by driving the green on the par-4 first hole, narrowly missing eagle and making a birdie. He would post a score of 65 on the round, defeating the then amateur Jack Nicklaus by two stokes and winning the championship.

Perhaps Palmer's leadership and courage are best represented by something that took place away from the golf course. In 1997 he was diagnosed with prostate cancer. In his typical style he stood up to the challenge of this foe as he had all others in his life. He took the challenge head-on and defeated the cancer. In a testament to his generosity of spirit, he used his own plight to urge others to have themselves checked often and remain diligent. Who knows how many lives Mr. Palmer may have saved?

It has become a cliché to refer to something that is the best as a "Cadillac." So it is somewhat ironic that Palmer is pictured with a Cadillac in that famous picture from 1973, for he is clearly in a class by himself. It can be debated whether Palmer was the greatest golfer of all time, but in my opinion, Arnold Palmer is definitely the greatest professional.

"What other people may find in poetry or art museums, I find in the flight of a good drive."

৵ Arnold Palmer

Cars and Pars

I was just settling into my seat on the plane when the cell phone rang. Flipping it open, I heard the voice on the other end begin to speak before I could even say hello.

"It must be nice. Yeah, it must be real nice to work in a job that you don't *hate*. I know you are on your way down to the PGA Show in Orlando, and I hope you catch a cold," chided my snowed-in friend.

The flight attendant's icy stare was even more foreboding than my friend's verbal lashing, so I answered his charge with a simple "I gotta go," and I was off to Orlando.

The long flight gave me a chance to reflect on my youthful dreams of a career in golf and sports media, and on how, over many years, circumstance and conviction have helped guide me through success and failure. From the mailroom to the *New York Times* best-seller list. From awesome NASCAR race tracks throughout the country to back here at the PGA Show, where in a few hours I will help broadcast the event to golfers everywhere.

Each January nearly 50,000 PGA professionals, golf buyers, VIPs, and media figures converge on the Orange County Convention Center in Orlando, Florida, for the annual PGA Merchandise Show. Over 1,200 vendors pack into the massive exhibition halls. If you were to walk every aisle at the "PGA Show" (as it is commonly known) then you would traverse nearly ten miles!

The sheer size of this show makes it clear how big the golf industry is, and how many people work to support the game. However, I am convinced that for every person at the show, there are literally thousands of people who would love to take their

"It's not how fast you get there, but how long you stay."

⤳ Patty Berg

places and get a job in a field that they are passionate about. This chapter takes a look at the path I took into not only a career in golf but also the world of NASCAR, and how a similar approach might work for you to break into your dream job.

I have been attending the show for most of the last two decades. Most of those years were spent meeting with customers at the show when I worked in private-label manufacturing of golf equipment, having developed and built products for companies such as Wilson, RAM, Lynx, MacGregor, Northwestern, and Nicklaus, among others. Each year I am amazed at the scale and variety of products available. I am even more impressed with the sophistication of the yearly crop of new high-tech and high-performance golf equipment. To me, the PGA Show is golf's fifth major, at least on the business side of the game.

While I attended the show for many years as a golf industry executive, for the last few years I have been there as a business reporter for The Golf Channel. In 2005 I cohosted six hours of live coverage with Kelly Tilghman, Adam Barr, and the rest of the Golf Channel cast. The Golf Channel reaches over 85 million people all over the world. What a thrill it was to broadcast to millions of golfers and give them a glimpse of all of the exciting new products. It was the first time that The Golf Channel had broadcast live from the show, and six hours is a lot of television time to fill. While our producers, directors, camera operators, and technical support staff no doubts carried the lion's share of the workload, I can tell you that on the broadcast side it was pure fun.

My primary role on The Golf Channel is to explain the technology in new golf equipment. However, I have been able to use my forum of exposure to highlight other stories that I thought were important. One of those stories took place this last summer. Arnold Palmer was in Rhode Island for a golf tournament hosted by Brad Faxon and Billy Andrade. The Golf Channel was broadcasting the event, and I was assigned to cover it. While there, Mr. Palmer put aside some time to discuss a new initiative that he was involved in through one of his sponsors. The new Palmer initia-

"You are what you think you are, in golf and in life."

∽ Raymond Floyd

tive was to get people to quit smoking. Smoking is the number-one cause of preventable death in America. I was captivated by the idea that one of the biggest names in the game's history would lend his credibility and influence to such a cause. I decided that it was a story that needed the widest possible audience, and I decided to produce a feature on it for Golf Central. My theme was to take a close look at the interwoven histories of smoking and the game of golf at the highest levels. As you may know, there was a time when virtually all of the top players in the game were also smokers. Mr. Palmer was gracious and accommodating as always, and his message was clear: *I stopped smoking before it killed me, and so can you.* The feature aired the next night, and the response I received was overwhelming. I have had many opportunities to host television features about things that I thought were interesting, humorous, or important, but never had I had the opportunity to carry a message that could possibly save a life. I called the feature "Arnie's New Army."

Less than two weeks later, two of my books were published: the third *Chicken Soup for the Soul* book that I coauthored with Jack Canfield and Mark Victor Hansen, and my second book specifically about NASCAR, called the *NASCAR Xtreme Race Journal for Kids*. This book was a follow-up to our 2003 release *Chicken Soup for the NASCAR Soul*, which has become the best-selling NASCAR book of all time. In producing these books I worked directly with some of the biggest names in the sport, including Jeff Gordon, Tony Stewart, and Michael Waltrip. I found the NASCAR drivers to be some the nicest and most grounded professional athletes I have ever worked with.

I love the pace, variety, passion, and intensity of working in exciting and vastly different arenas. My reason for recounting this is to demonstrate the fact that you can make a career out of your favorite hobbies. People like to assume that if you have a fascinating career, you got it either through luck or connections, but that is not true in my case. I created the career I enjoy through relentless persistence, discipline, and adherence to my master plan. Oftentimes this kind of pursuit involves some very

"If I had to cram all my tournament experience into one sentence, I would say, 'Don't give up and don't let up!'"

↝ Tony Lema

lonely hours filled with doubt as failures and setbacks work to wear down your convictions. Such was the case with me, and I suspect virtually everyone else, who has had a job that is commonly addressed with a statement beginning with "It must be nice . . ."

There are countless ways to break into any industry, but here are the steps that I took and that I recommend to my clients who want to get a job in golf, or NASCAR, or really any other field.

First of all, forget about the money. I know that sounds foolish, but for right now, put your concerns about money aside (we will get back to it). To get into the field that you want, it usually takes sacrifice and no small measure of paying your dues. For my part, my media career began working as a stringer, for no pay, for local AM radio stations while I was in high school in Connecticut. I would cover a local basketball, football, or hockey game in the evening. The next morning I was up at 4:00 A.M., and I would be at the radio station by 5:00 A.M. to cut my feature, then it was off to school. This exercise gave me a vast amount of experience. Since my efforts were not costing the station any money, they were liberal in allowing me to cover a wide variety of events that captured my interest. In those early years I covered virtually every sport in the area, including National Hockey League games (the Hartford Whalers) and the Sammy Davis Jr. Greater Hartford Open on the PGA Tour. I can remember seeing the people I interviewed, such as professional athletes, Sammy Davis Jr., Bob Hope, and countless others looking at me and no doubt wondering how this kid who looked like he was twelve even got on the grounds. But it was a wonderful experience, and a testament to the value of using other people's motivation to get what they need (sports content on the radio) as an advantage in realizing your plan (gaining experience).

I continued my work in radio throughout my college years, and when I graduated I landed a job in the mail room at ESPN. I made sure that I was always the first one in and the last one to leave each night. If a job was awful and no one else wanted it, that was the assignment I volunteered for. Within two months I was promoted to a job in the production department, where my assignments were the NHL, NFL, and SportsCenter.

I was with ESPN for two years, until I had an opportunity to turn my passion for the game of golf into a career and started to work in golf equipment manufacturing.

There are some important points to consider when you read this account and plan your own path for attaining the job or career you have always wanted. Remember that you are likely one of thousands who want the job. Do your homework, and give your prospective employer a better reason to hire you than "I love sports." Learn everything you can about the industry and the company. Try to make contact with an executive within the particular company you want to join, and ask that executive if you can take ten minutes of his or her time in a phone interview. You will be amazed at how accommodating people can be *if you only ask.*

Next, do not let discouragement or rejection stop you. It is common, when you are trying to break in, to face massive rejection. I did, and so does everyone else. The problem is that for many people, that is when they stop trying. They allow someone else's opinion of their value to determine how they value themselves. Don't do it. You know how good you are, even if the world has not realized it yet.

One of the best and most successful methods I recommend for breaking into sports and in particular into the golf industry is to volunteer at tournaments and charity events. They are always looking for good people to help them run these events, and it is a great way to get experience and meet the right people. Be sure to take full advantage of the opportunity. Over-deliver in everything you do, and make sure that you are the best they ever had in whatever area they assign you. Go out of your way to meet everyone you possibly can, and arrange to meet with them after the event is over to sit down and talk about the event and how they run it. This is an excellent way to work yourself into a job, and I have used it with countless clients who are working their dream jobs today.

As to the important point of making money, which I put aside earlier, my feeling is as follows: The time you are spending "paying your dues" and getting to know the right people is worth the income you will be forgoing in the exercise. I realize you need to make money to live, however, to that end, my advice is to go out and get a second job and if necessary a third job. Try to find jobs in areas that also pique your interest or can help to support your long-term goals.

It may take time, sacrifice, creativity, tenacity, and most of all hard work to attain your dream job, but if you have the unyielding conviction that you will make it happen, then one day people will be telling you, "It must be nice . . ."

"The game is meant to be fun."

⌇ Jack Nicklaus

17

Enjoying the Round of Your Life

༄

Go Low, Mo

Mo Norman was not a stranger to breaking course records. The eccentric Canadian pro has been called the purest ball-striker of all time.

In 1948 Norman scored one of his more distinctive course records. Distinctive, that is, if it had been accomplished by anyone else other than Mo Norman.

Coming to the final hole, Norman needed only a four to make par and break the record. On the tee, his playing partner looked at the hole and declared that it was a "driver–9-iron hole." Norman absorbed the information, only he reversed the recipe. Norman proceeded to hit his 9-iron into the fairway; then from there he pured his driver off the deck to within one foot of the hole. He made birdie and broke the course record by two shots.

"Keep your sense of humor. There's enough stress in the rest of your life to let bad shots ruin a game you're supposed to enjoy."

᠅ Amy Alcott

His Way

Frank Sinatra was one of the greatest entertainers and personalities of the twentieth century. However, one distinction Mr. Sinatra did not have was that of being a great golfer.

During his first round of golf with Arnold Palmer, the "Chairman of the Board" spent most of his time laboring through the thick rough on the Palm Springs golf course they were playing.

After posting a huge score, Sinatra, asked Palmer what he thought about "Ol' Blue Eyes' golf game." Palmer, who need not bow to any man, smiled and replied, "Not bad, but I still prefer golf."

"Always keep it fun. If you don't have fun, you'll never grow as a person or a player."

∻ Tiger Woods

꒜

Calling His Shot

Babe Ruth had a long love affair with golf that nearly mirrored his passion for baseball. At the end of the 1931 season, after Ruth had hit 46 home runs, driven in 163, and averaged .373, he informed the media that the greatest accomplishment of the year had been a round of 73 at his home course on Long Island.

Once, while he was on vacation in Bermuda, the Babe's love of the game, his supreme confidence, and the fickle nature of golf all collided. Ruth stood at the tee on the par-4, 370-yard fifteenth hole at the Mid-Ocean Club, surveying his tee shot options. His caddie pleaded with him to lay up in front of a pond that protected the green. Ruth, who never backed down to any challenge, demanded his driver, claiming that he could throw the ball on the green from where he stood. Perhaps he would have been better served throwing the ball to the green, for he proceeded to dunk the next fifteen balls into the water.

Enraged, Ruth broke his club in half and marched into the clubhouse.

"Go out and have fun. Golf is a game for everyone, not just for the talented few."

~ Harvey Penick

꒰꒱

The Merry Mex

Is there any man who appeared to have more fun on a golf course than Lee Trevino?

Lee Trevino, known as the "Merry Mex," has always been a favorite of the galleries. Trevino is a tenacious competitor, but from his earliest days of professional golf he developed an entertaining routine that helped him keep stress at bay and concentrate on the task at hand. Trevino would talk and laugh almost constantly. His fun and enthusiasm were infectious.

At the 1971 U.S. Open at Merion, Trevino was preparing to tee off against Jack Nicklaus in an eighteen-hole play-off. Feeling the effect from nerves, Trevino looked for a way to diminish the stress. He remembered that his daughter had left a plastic snake in his golf bag. The funny-man Trevino pulled the snake out and tossed it at Nicklaus. While Nicklaus' reaction would have most likely defined the propriety of Trevino's act, Nicklaus laughed and so did Trevino, the gallery, and the rest of the golf world (Nicklaus would later admit that he had seen the snake in Trevino's bag, so he was expecting it to make an appearance).

Trevino would go on to post a three-stroke victory over Nicklaus and win his second U.S. Open championship.

⌁

Enjoying the Round of Your Life

All human beings have an innate capacity for happiness. What's more, it is human nature to seek happiness, to be at one with the world, to feel at peace.

I believe that is why we love the game of golf—it not only challenges us mentally and physically, but also helps us to aspire to the ideal of happiness.

While happiness takes different forms in different people, there is one thing that is for certain: our world blooms when we are not constrained by stress, anxiety, and worry. We feel better physically, our minds gain clarity, productivity goes through the roof, and our relationships become deeper and more fulfilling (because we are more enjoyable to be around). In short, we start to have fun.

I have a friend who begins every round with the same irreverent ritual. Right before the first tee ball is struck, which he makes sure is done by someone other than him, he will declare "Stop! Stop! I almost forgot."

He will then proceed, quite dramatically, to dig deeply into his bag and pull out a golf ball, which he will hold high above his head while he marches toward the pond between the tee area and the first fairway. He then mutters something like "Ooga, booga" and tosses the ball into the water.

The routine is best observed in a foursome with at least one person who has never seen him do this before, because that person does not know whether to laugh or run the other way. Invariably, either I or someone else that knows the routine will admit that my friend was making a preemptive sacrifice to the "Golf Gods" in the hope that they will go easy on us. Corny, yes, but it certainly takes away the first-tee shot apprehension and tension (especially if one of us proceeds to dunk the tee shot anyway).

The funny thing about happiness, like so many other aspects of mental posture, it is a *choice*. You can *choose* to enjoy the time and place, or you can *choose* to overreact to everything, take it all too seriously, and be miserable. Have you noticed that problems seem to compound themselves when we overreact to them? How often have you heard about a player slamming his putter after a missed putt and breaking it? Now he has to finish out the round putting with his 3-wood. Problems compounded.

If our reactions surround us with negative energy, then the only thing we can possibly expect is negative consequences. We are overcome by our own seriousness.

I have noticed this overdependency on seriousness quite often in young golfers who have reached a proficient if not excellent level of ability in the game. Either through self-expectation or through the influence of pressures outside of themselves, such as those coming from parents or coaches, they have come to believe that they should hit every shot with precise perfection. They have not yet realized that golf is a game that is negotiated, not dominated. That golf by its very nature is about overcoming our mistakes, not becoming upset at their arrival, for it is inevitable that they shall come. They simply take themselves too seriously, feeling that a sour scowl should be worn as a badge after every round as a mark of aspiring to perfection.

Allowing ourselves to have fun on the golf course, to embrace humor, allows us to view things with perspective. It helps us to keep our focus and concentration. It keeps nerves and anxiety at bay.

Yes, as golf is a human game, mistakes will happen. Being able to laugh at a situation will open the opportunity to learn from it without our minds becoming shut down through rage.

It is important also to realize that while having the ability to laugh at your mistakes is part of the maturing process of great

"If our reactions surround us with negative energy, then the only thing we can possibly expect is negative consequences."

golfers, self-directed humor is never self-demeaning. Remember that you are what you tell yourself, and the fact that you do not hit every shot perfectly does not mean that you are a golfing failure. Watch the best golfers in the world and see how many of the top players answer a missed shot with a wry smile and a shake of the head, while those who miss the cut tighten up and begin cursing the world (and themselves).

We all could stand to be a little less serious in our lives. Life's little inconveniences are part of being human. Heavy traffic, deadlines looming, a crowded train, coffee stains on your tie, or a million other petty inconveniences are inevitable. We can choose to allow them to tie us up in knots and diminish our attitude, productivity, likableness, and health or we can put them into their proper perspective.

So, let's all have a little more fun, because isn't that what this round of life is all about?

I think at that time I really fell in love with the game. I'd always loved golf, but now it was a new type of love that I could have."

    ⤳ Tom Watson, after
        winning the 1977 Open
        Championship

18

A Lifelong Journey

جᢒ

THE PERFECT GIFT

My father was impossible to buy gifts for. It's not that he was unappreciative when you gave him one, it was just that he had gotten to the age where if there was anything he needed, he either already had it, or he would simply go out and get it. So, after an endless parade of ties, I set out to find a special gift that would really touch him.

Golf and hockey were my dad's passions, and while his days on blades were fading into a distant memory, his love of golf continued to grow. In many ways dad was your typical senior golfer. His power fade had steadily developed into a livable if distance-robbing slice. But, it wasn't good to let his swing fool you (my brothers and I called it the "stepping in the bucket swing" due to an errant left foot during his follow-through). My dad was a highly successful CPA, and he could read the slippery greens at the Ridgewood Country Club in Danbury, Connecticut, like he was reading a balance sheet. This and a steely-eyed determination won him more matches than he lost.

I had been working the golf club equipment industry for a few years and decided that I would surprise my dad with a new set

"*Golf is twenty percent mechanics and technique. The other eighty percent is philosophy, humor, tragedy, romance, melodrama, companionship, camaraderie, cussedness, and conversation.*"

⚬ Grantland Rice

of golf clubs when he and mom visited my wife Donna and me in Orlando, during their winter vacation.

One of the larger golf club shaft manufacturers had just introduced a new steel shaft made especially for senior golfers that featured more "kick" through impact, resulting in more distance. The only problem was that I had to make sure I never told my father that the set featured "senior flex" golf shafts, for fear that I might offend some delicate sensibilities. So I wrapped the shafts with a shaft band that simply said "Dynamic" (a term used in the industry to describe a method of measurement of consistency from one shaft to another). My father was delighted to receive his new set, and we planned to play that very day.

Dad made me explain every nuance of the set: the offset, the weight distribution, even the design concept. When it came to the steel shafts I simply and confidently proclaimed them as "Dynamics," as if that alone would explain their story. He did not challenge me.

My father's day on the links was fantastic, but not because he was knocking down pins. You see, with these new shafts, he was hitting the ball longer than he had in years and loving every minute of it. I remember one shot where he was about 115 to 120 yards from an elevated green. My dad chose an 8-iron as he had a million times before and promptly fired the shot directly at the pin, going long by only twenty yards. This continued all day, and it was probably one of the most exciting and enjoyable rounds we ever played, as each shot was a new discovery of hitherto foregone power.

That afternoon my mother and father flew back to their New England home. Exactly eleven days later my father passed away from a massive heart attack. In spite of the grief, my heavy heart was lighter thinking about that magic day we shared on the golf course, one last time, when I finally found the perfect gift.

It was a gift that made my father's final round a joy. However, it pales in comparison to the gift of the game that he gave me.

Some gifts really are perfect.

Through the Footsteps of Time

The men crouched behind low stone walls. Musket fire pierced the air above their heads, randomly seeking the warm flesh of the unlucky one who happened in its path. Worse off yet were the sorry souls cut down by cannon fire, the evil spheres that caused the demise of multiple patriots with every blast.

It is hard to imagine the angst, the fear, and the nobility of the brave soldiers who squared off on this rocky slope.

I was flooded with emotion as I strode down the majestic fairways of the Carnegie Abbey Course in Portsmouth, Rhode Island. On a perfect New England spring day, I was playing golf with new friends Don, Patrick, and Bill. We had just hit our drives on the tight, slightly dogleg left, par-4 sixth hole. I was struck by a sight of a Colonial-era graveyard surrounded by massive stones, stones that for hundreds of years had silently stood as sentries for the confines of its eternal occupants. While the inscriptions were moving, I found it even more fascinating that this noble sight must have sat in near obscurity for two centuries before its liberation from the scrub brush by the artistic stroke of the golf course architect.

Describing my emotions to Bill, he was quick to note that directly beneath us, less than twenty yards off the tee, was the final resting place for forty former slaves who had lived and farmed the property during part of its long history.

As we approached our drives, I turned to Manny, my caddie, to express my reverence for this special place, and Manny informed me that far more was to come. On cue, Bill explained that this beautiful, rolling property on Narragansett Bay was the location of numerous confrontations during the American Revolution. Specifically, the hole we were playing was the very sight of the

"Battle of Bloody Run," where estimates are that five hundred to two thousand men had lost their lives and were buried beneath the ground we strode.

I stood for a minute in awe, consumed by the thought that a place that was now so beautiful could have been the site of such violence.

I can never remember feeling on a golf course the way I did that day. Part of me felt out of place, as if I were violating this land that still belonged to the hearts, sounds, and emotions of its past. Another part of me felt a true reverence, a sense of common union with this spot and an appreciation for the people who had been there before me.

That is when it hit me.

How wonderful is this game of golf that since a course designer used this land as the canvas upon which a beautiful and challenging golf course would unfold, a piece of history would be freed from decades of overgrowth? I will admit that I did not know a thing at that time about the "Battle of Bloody Run," much less the actual spot where the battle took place. But I have a deep appreciation for it now.

Thanks to Carnegie Abbey Golf Course, the efforts and sacrifices of these brave men would not be lost to obscurity, but would be remembered and forever celebrated because of numerous historical markings and environmental sensitivity.

I love the game of golf, not only for its dignity and camaraderie, but also because every now and then the game becomes a vehicle to explore and appreciate something deeper, such as, on this day, a garden memorial to the people who gave so much so that we may enjoy the moment.

꒰

A Lifelong Journey

My father instilled in me a love for the game of golf.

I do not recall the first time I swung a golf club, but I remember deciding that golf was a game I wanted to play when I was about fifteen. Since then, I have wondered many times whether my game's recurrent slice is something instilled into my genes at a molecular level.

An emotion that I clearly remember from those early days was, as a small kid, striding awkwardly, laboring under the weight of my dad's old leather golf bag, how mad I would get at myself for not learning the game a lot earlier in life.

This sensation was accentuated as I watched my friends, who seemingly had learned the game fresh from the womb, crushing (well, I thought at the time it was long) drive after drive with their persimmon drivers while I searched the weeds for my wayward orb.

My father played a slice for as long as I can remember, and, for a long time, I thanked him for generously imparting that part of his game to me. What my dad really taught me to appreciate were the more esoteric aspects of the game, those elements that are not played out in the form of 300-yard drives or birdie putts from down town. My father taught me that golf is a lifelong love affair. It begins with an infatuation, develops into a senseless love, and matures into a contentious, maddening, frustrating, exhilarating, fulfilling, and yet understanding kind of bond you see in an elderly couple in the park.

It is difficult to describe why the addicting game of golf is so endearing. I believe it is because the game allows us a glimpse of perfection. How often have you endured a horrible round, replete with proclamations of quitting the game, only to be saved by that one miraculous shot that keeps you coming back?

While that shot may not come with the same frequency for most of us as it does for the finest golfers in the world, the game does not discriminate in allowing our aspirations to perfection. Why, a first-time golfer could sink a sixty-foot triple breaker or chip in for par. Each of us has the capacity to hit a shot with the same results as the best the game has ever known.

What's more, golf allows us the opportunity to sometimes perform those feats on the *same* golf course walked by the game's legends. What other sport would allow such an experience?

Of course, the ultimate glimpse of perfection in golf is represented by the hole in one. Perhaps this is why it is so celebrated. The ace is the rarest of feats and yet so consummate. It is singular; it stands alone; it is *one.*

In our quest to master a game that cannot be mastered, golf is foremost about self-discovery. A person is revealed to the world in a round of golf. Even more so, we are revealed to ourselves. Our character, integrity, and morality are all put to the test, and our ability to handle pressure is put to the fire. Sometimes we succeed, sometimes we fail, and if we are observant, each time we learn something new, something to keep us coming back.

It is for all these reasons, and more, that golf is a game mirroring life. Golf is both a mystical journey of joy and sorrow and a physical journey of cause and effect. It is a game providing us with opportunities for wonderfully torturous choices—take a chance and achieve supreme glory or wallow in dismal failure—always with the promise of another day to try again.

To be a golfer is to be an optimist, for we all believe that our next round will be better than our last. We are always striving for more. In fact, it is the game's elusive nature that makes it all the more appealing. Ultimately, the game leaves us with more questions than answers and presents a fascinating dichotomy that keeps golf fresh and new despite its ancient origins.

My dad was right. Golf truly is like a love affair, a journey of a lifetime.

About Matthew E. Adams

Matthew Adams is a *New York Times* and *USA Today* best-selling author, a golf television personality, a golf equipment expert, and a highly sought-after professional speaker. Adams' writing has appeared in newspapers and magazines throughout America, including the *Los Angeles Times*. Adams began his career working in the production department at ESPN, where his assignments were the NHL, the NFL, and Sports Center. Adams followed his passion for the game to work in the golf equipment manufacturing industry for over fifteen years in sales, design, sourcing, and private-label production for some of the biggest brands in the industry. For the last five years Adams has devoted much of his time to golf course operations consulting. Adams can be seen weekly on The Golf Channel in addition to his syndicated product reviews and his columns on www.FairwaysOfLife.com. In addition to *Fairways of Life*, Adams was a coauthor of *Chicken Soup for the Soul of America*, which benefited the New York Area Relief Fund; *Chicken Soup for the NASCAR Soul*, the best-selling NASCAR book of all time; *The NASCAR Xtreme Race Journal for Kids*, which was published in 2005; and the *Fast and Lean Racing Cookbook*, which will come to the market in 2006. Adams is a dynamic and inspiring speaker who is available for your next function. To receive more information on how to book Matthew Adams, please contact his agents:

Speaking:

> Eddie Smith, President
> Golf Podium
> 5500 Military Trail, Ste. 22-294
> Jupiter, FL 33458
> (866) 567-4653
> esmith@golfpodium.com
> www.golfpodium.com

Broadcast/Literary:

> Alan Sanders
> 4 Linda Lane
> Katonah, NY 10536
> (914) 248-8828
> alansanders@optonline.net

For all other correspondence, e-mail Matthew Adams' office at: FairwaysOfLife@cox.net or visit www.FairwaysOfLife.com

Please note that due to volume, Matthew Adams does not personally read all of his e-mail, and most requests are handled by the office staff.

꒐

About www.FairwaysOfLife.com

Due to the overwhelming response to this book, Matthew Adams established a website, www.FairwaysOfLife.com, in order to give the legions of devoted fans of *Fairways Of Life* a portal for a deeper, even more inspiring experience with his work and the game of golf, as well as a place to share ideas and learn about new *Fairways of Life* projects.